AND *He* STILL
*Hears*

# AND *He* STILL *Hears*

Compiled By:
Trena Stephenson

Publisher:
Daughters of Distinction

"And He Still Hears"
Published by Daughters of Distinction

15122 Callohan Ct
Silver Springs, MD 20906 USA

Copyright © 2010 DOFDLLC
Daughters Of Distiniction

All rights reserved. No part of the book may be reproduced in any form without permission in writing from the publisher, except in the case of brief quotations embodied in articles or reviews

Cover Design and Layout: Sarah Thompson
Interior Layout: Ebony Richardson
Editorial: Cynthia D. Thomas

## *Acknowledgements*

With Many Thanks,

First and foremost I would like to thank God for being my creator and my all in all. To my beautiful daughter who I love dearly, thanks for the love and support you give continually. To my parents and my extended family thanks for being there when I needed you the most. To WofGod Inc. staff and affiliates thanks so much for all you do to hold my arms up I couldn't do what I do without you. To my Daughters of Distinction staff you all rock thanks for all you do now we can breathe a little, don't get to comfortable though the ride is just beginning. To Rev. Jamar Suber of Suber Media Group LLC., thanks so much for being my advisor on this project it is so appreciated. To my Apostle June A. Hunter thanks for your support. To the two awesome women of God who did the forward and review of this book, Apostle Dr. Elizabeth Harriston of Women With A Call International and Apostle Veter Nichols of Veter Nichols Ministries, your contribution to this project is so appreciated. Last but not least thanks to all my co-authors of this book, I am so Godly proud of you the best is yet to come for each and every one of you. God stretched us and made us better vessels of honor for his sake. If I have forgotten anyone charge to my head and not my heart thank you, thank you, thank you.

With Love

Trena

## *Foreword*

Prophet Trena has brought her readers into a place of understanding that prayer can be both challenging and rewarding. The scriptural approach provides opportunity for prayer warriors to develop prayer bible studies where prayer and the bible can meet in an effective manner. This would allow a platform for the prayer group to discuss their concerns and praise report in a corporate setting. As many people through the years have waited for prayers to be answered, how refreshing it is to know of God's power and willingness to answer our prayers. This explosive and challenging book prompts us to say with great confidence that "He Still Hears".

Elizabeth A. Hairston-McBurrows B.A.,M.A./M.F.A D.B.S, Ph.D.
Amelia Hairston
"Continuing the Royal Legacy"

## *Preface*

I believe that meeting Prophetess Trena was a God moment. A set season that was so divine. As I looked into this woman of God's eyes that Sunday afternoon in Virginia there was an instant connection. I saw the love of God and a woman so filled with Godly wisdom and counsel needing to be released to the "Nation of Women" of the earth. This book bespeaks her nature, character, love for people, and her true desire to see God's people totally free. There is a fresh anointing for deliverance available through the reading of this book. It is a weapon in the hand of any believer.

Prophetess Trena and the women of power that penned the pages are last day "Deborah's", called to walk along side of God's men to set Christ body free through faithfulness, honesty, integrity, and transparency. We endeavor to challenge this generation coming behind us to follow the wisdom of those who have laid a foundation of listening for the voice of the Father, for He still listens and speaks.

As you delve into the pages of this book you will literally hear the voice of the Father responding back to you. Many times without us even mentioning our pain to Him, he hears us through those painful and distressful moments and seasons. He's listening when you can't speak. The Father hears your tears when your voice is silent.

This book is setting a precedent for healing and deliverance. It is going to help many women, and I believe also men, to find their story because of the honesty and transparency of the testimonies of these great leaders in Christendom. Leaders who have dared to open up and tell their stories. You see, when leaders open up and show the dark painful secrets of their lives to the world, it helps all of us who have dark painful secrets in our lives to begin to feel free to open up and "dare to release." Often times we feel God is so "high and lofty" that He cannot be touched with the feelings of our infirmities; so we don't talk to Him. We won't share our pain with Him. You cannot touch God without Him touching you back and we do not just touch Him with our worship alone, we can also touch Him with our pain and infirmities.

Before you delve through the pages of this book, I want you to begin to open up your heart and your mouth. Be prepared to speak to God with all honesty and sincerity. Decide to do it now because Daddy God hears you. He won't reject you, leave, or forsake you. He promised us that through His word He is listening for the sound of your voice; the sound of your pain, and the sound of your tears. He hears all of it. Don't be afraid. David said it so well in Psalms 56:3, "When I am afraid, I will trust in you." So when you are afraid and you think God is not listening, just trust in Him and you will see Him manifest His presence in a very loving and fatherly way. He will hear you and heal you. Your years ahead will be filled with blessings and goodness because He listens and hears.

Prophetess Trena has certainly heard from God with this book. It is and will be one of the most unique written for this generation. Those who have journeyed ahead of you have paved a legacy and that is "God still hears." He listens and always brings change. Remember what the women in this book have learned, "that your light afflictions are for a moment, but they produce in you a more excellent weight of glory."

When you complete this read you will be set free. What He has in His heart for us is a future and a Hope. He has an expected end; so therefore, God has ordained that you prosper and be in health, even as your soul experiences prosperity. I am honored to have been asked to be a part of this excellent ministry work.

Apostle (Mother) Veter Nichols
Founder, Covenant Fellowship
Founder, Elijah to Elisha School of Wisdom and Mentoring of the Fold Ministry Gifts
Senior Pastor, New Covenant Life Ministries International Church

# Table of Contents

Father Do You Hear Me? ........................................................... 13

What To Do While You Wait ..................................................... 19

Patience Brings Forth The Promise ........................................... 27

Does He Know? ........................................................................ 37

Does He Care?
"The Power of Empathy" ........................................................... 45

What's In Your Heart? ............................................................... 51

Be Still And Know ..................................................................... 61

Stop Trippin! ............................................................................. 71

Holiness Is Required ................................................................. 79

Operating Under An Open Heaven ........................................... 87

Unstopping The Blockages ....................................................... 95

And He Still Hears .................................................................... 105

How it all began ....................................................................... 115

SADIQA'S PLACE:
A HOUSE OF HOPE (SPAHOH) ............................................. 117

# Chapter 1

## Father Do You Hear Me?

Do you ever sit back and wonder if you are being heard? Or paid attention to? Do you just sit back and wonder, is there anybody really listening to what you have to say.

Have you ever had a conversation with someone in which you were pouring out your heart's cry and they showed no interest at all or did not respond back to you? Did you say to yourself or even cry out loud, "DO YOU HEAR ME? ARE YOU LISTENING TO WHAT I AM SAYING?"

Well, today I just want to share with you my heart's story about wondering whether God was listening to my cry, prayers, and groaning. I was in rough place in my life. It seemed as if I was left alone to deal with some rough situations by myself. I might as well keep this real with you; I wanted to know if God was truly listening to me. I wanted to know if He was truly inclining His ear unto me, and paying attention to what I was saying.

Sometimes we can find ourselves in a place where it seems as if we are all alone. It seems as if no one even cares what we are going through. Sometimes we feel like God has forsaken us and left us to our own devices. The word of God reminds us that He promised that He would never leave or forsake us (Hebrews 13:5

King James Version KJV). If we are honest with ourselves, we must admit that we all have allowed the enemy of our soul to play on our emotions. The enemy tries to make us feel as if our Heavenly Father has abandoned us.

About 2 years ago, I lost my job while living in St. Louis. This caused a string of things to begin to take place. Eventually I even lost my apartment. I ended living in the church for about 3 months. I married a man who I should not have married and all hell broke loose.

My life was in a tailspin. I was having a hard time trying to find employment. My husband wasn't working and we begin to lose things. The list goes on and on. I cried, I prayed, I prayed and I cried until at one point I hollered out "FATHER DO YOU HEAR ME?"

I was in distress and wanted to know if He was listening to me. I wanted to know if He was truly paying attention to my situation. It was very frustrating and sometimes I wanted to just say forget it, this is useless and He is not listening to me anyway, so why bother. But I kept being reminded that I could not give up now just because the road is getting a little tough. I was reminded by fellow laborers in the gospel and even the word of God that I could not just give up and throw in the towel. If I had done so, I would have given the enemy just what he wanted. So, I kept calling out to Him both day and night and reminding him of His word.

"Lord, you said that in my distress, I can cry unto you and you will hear me."(Psalm 120:1 KJV). What is going on Lord, where are you? *"Lord, your word told me that if I call on you in the day of trouble that you would be a very present help in the time of trouble."* (Psalm 46:1 KJV).
How come you are not answering me? Yes, I went there, because I knew that if I had not continued to call upon Him, I would have backslid and that's just keeping it real.

It seemed that everyone around was being blessed and

having their prayers answered but me. I asked God, Lord, what is going on? What am I doing or not doing that I should be doing. Why are you are not answering me? FATHER DO YOU HEAR ME? What's going on? Why does it seem as if you are far, far away? Come on Jesus; don't leave me out here like this. I need your help and I need it now!

While going through my boisterous storm and not seeing my way clear, I found myself crying out, "My God, my God, why hast thou forsaken me?" Jesus had uttered this very dreadful cry on the cross. As a result He bore our sins and diseases in His own body and took our judgment allowing His heavenly father withdrew His holy and intimate presence. Jesus was forsaken by God because he suffered in our place, having become a curse for God. Jesus was also claiming the entire psalm as a description of Himself simply by uttering this verse. This became my daily prayer and my midnight's cry: *"My God, my God, why has thou forsaken me? Why art thou so far from helping me, and from the words of my roaring? Oh my God, I cry in the daytime, but thou hearest not: and in the night season, and am not silent."*(Psalm 22:1-2 KJV).

Beloved, like Jesus Himself, we may at times feel forsaken by God. When this occurs, hold fast to the revelation of God's love and goodness toward you. Continue to pray and to trust Him no matter what it looks like. Continue to cry out to Him with everything you got. Hear me when I call, *"O God of my righteousness: thou hast enlarged me when I was in distress; have mercy upon me, and hear my prayer."*(Psalms 4:1 KJV). In order for this scripture to become a reality for me, I had to make sure that my relationship with God was in order. I had to ensure that I was living as holy as possible, bore no ill-will towards anyone and maintained compassion or in my heart. Our prayers can be hindered and not answered if we are holding on to revenge, jealousy resentment and bitterness. We want to make sure that we are walking in love at all times. Is it always easy? No, but it can be done.

*"If I regard iniquity in my heart, the Lord will not hear me: But verily God hath heard me; he hath attended to the voice of my prayer. Blessed be God, which hath not turned away my prayer, not his mercy from me."*(Psalm 66:18-20 KJV).

I discovered that in order to have assurance that God will answer our call for help; we must sincerely endeavor to live a godly lifestyle. Even while going through my trials and tribulations, I still had to maintain my relationship with God. I still had to preach and teach in the midst of the storm and even while asking Him, "FATHER DO YOU HEAR ME?"

Be encouraged this day to know that our Heavenly Father does here us when we call. However we have to make sure that our relationship with Him is where it needs to be. I thank God for hearing my cry and my supplications unto Him regarding my situation. He made a way for me to come out of the storm. I had to go through it wondering if he was really listening to me and could He even hear me. *"I called upon His name out of a low dungeon."*(Lamentations 3:55 KJV). I was so low, that I didn't even think that God Himself could hear me. He did and I am forever grateful to Him for hearing my despairing cry. Now, I can boldly say:

*"But thou, O Lord, art a shield for me; my glory, and the lifter of mine head. I cried unto the Lord with my voice, and he heard me out of his holy hill."*(Psalm 3:3-4 KJV).

I now know that He is still here and never left me. I now know that He is still on my side and hears and answers my prayers. I now know that He will never leave me or forsake because I am His and He is all mine. I now know that in my distress, I can be like David and proclaim "This poor woman cried, and the Lord has heard me, and saved me out of all my troubles. Hallelujah!" I can say thank you Jesus for delivering and answering me in my times of distress. I thank you forgiving ear unto my cry and hearing me when I call you.

Beautiful women of God, let us endeavor to make sure that

we are in right relationship with God so that our prayers can be answered. The word of God reminds us to:

*"Confess your faults one to another, and pray one for another, that ye may be healed. The effectual fervent prayer of the righteous man availeth much."*(James 5:16 KJV).

Let us walk in the spirit of humility and love so that our prayers can be answered and to know that He still hears.

## About The Author

Pastor Towana R. Clark

*Pastor Towana R. Clark currently resides in Capitol Heights, MD. Pastor Clark is founder/director of Divinely Inspired Victorious Achievers of God (DIVAS of God), ministry network that empowers women to achieve their divine purpose in God. She serves as associate pastor at True Believer's Pentecostal Glorious Church of God, where Apostle Ernest Quick, Jr. is Overseer and Sr. Pastor in Washington, DC.*

# Chapter 2

## What To Do While You Wait?

"*But they that wait upon the Lord shall renew their strength: they shall mount up with wings as eagles: they shall run, and not be weary: and they shall walk, and not faint.*"(Isaiah.40:31 KJV).

Funk & Wagnall's: Standard College Dictionary defines waiting as the act of one who waits; waiting in attendance; or that waits expecting! You are right there with the Lord, as your escort, trusting in him to be there for you. Do you remember how it was on that first real date? Remember being picked up by your "escort" having him open the car door for you, taking your hand and helping you into the car. When you arrived at your destination point, he got out, walked around to your side of the car, opened your door and took your hand to help you out of the car. He was attune to your every need while out for the evening. This is what the Lord does for us while we are waiting, He attunes to our every need.

While we are waiting, we are in a state of "Expectation", looking for the end of this test. The Bible tells us to *"Hold fast the profession of our faith without wavering; for he is faithful that promised."*(Hebrews 10:23 KJV) *"There hath no temptation taken you but such as is common to man: but God is faithful, who will not suffer you to be tempted above that ye are able; but will with the temptation also make a way to escape, that ye may be able to bear it."* (1Corinthians.10:13 KJV). Some tests are short lived, but some that go on for years. When the Lord has a calling in our lives each level must be tested before we get to the next level. Sometimes we ask the Lord, Where are you? *"O Lord, how long shall I cry, and thou will not hear!"*(Habakkuk 1:2 KJV).

I can tell you that, waiting is not always easy.

*"Fear thou not; for I am with thee: be not dismayed; for I am thy God: I will strengthen thee; yea, I will help thee; yea, I will uphold thee with the right hand of my righteousness."*(Isiah.41:10 KJV).

I know about waiting through a test, or shall I say tests. Christ has taught me what to do while you wait. There is a test that I have been going through for twenty one years. During these twenty one years, another test came that has lasted for thirteen years. Presently, I am still in, and going through both of them. People of the most high God; believe me when I tell you that the God that I serve is keeping me. Sure there have been times when I have cried and asked the Lord why me. Even through my tests, His grace and mercy has never failed me. There were times I have said, Lord I have been in this battle so long I just do not know what to do, however he speaks to my heart, and I am able to go on.

One thing we must understand, during the test is to keep the Lord Jesus Christ before and with us. Stop saying what if, and start saying with Christ I can. Look to Jesus who knows where He is leading you. Don't look at the test and the time spent in it; look at the enormous God that is with us in this. *"He hath said, I will never leave thee, nor forsake thee."*(Hebrews.13:5 KJV). *"Trust the Lord with all your heart: do not depend on your own understanding. Seek his will in all you do, and he will show you which path to take."*(Proverbs.3:5-6 New Living Translation NLT).

As I said earlier there are tests that are short and some that last for years. How do we endure the test? The Lord has taught me, to trust Him, stay busy and occupied with the things of God. You have a calling in Christ. When we are set aside for the cause of Christ for kingdom building, we must prepare ourselves in devotional prayer; supplication in fasting, standing firm in our assigned calling. Seek the Lord for yourself in this matter, stay prayerful, being in devotional and supplication with Him. The devil will have you think sometimes you are alone; remember the Lord is always with us. Don't let the devil make you think that you are all alone! Stop! Exhale! Stand straight, without curve or bend in your faith and say, enemy

*"Greater is he that is in you (me), than he that is in the world."*
(I John 4:4 KJV).

Believe me beloved, as the scripture says, *"For if they do these things in a green tree, what shall be done in the dry?"*(Luke 23:31 KJV). This passage is speaking about is Jesus and us, the believer. The things Jesus Christ had to endure for us, we must arm ourselves like wise to endure for Christ to be seen and lifted up in our lives. There are things that we must go through to let us know the strength that lies within each of us.

Sometime we do things by habit. The spirit of God appears sometimes and stirs us up in our walk with Him, to get us where He desires of us to go. The reason we read our word, and pray, is to be strong in Christ. Remember, God is our companion in our wait.

*"But now, O Israel, the lord who created you says,*
*"Do not be afraid, for I have ransomed you. I have called you by name: you are mine."*(Isaiah 43:1 NLT).
The Lord is preparing you for kingdom work. He is preparing you for greatness in Him. If we must die to the flesh as Christ died for us, let us prepare our minds and our spirits for waiting on the Lord in our tests. Every time we labor while we wait, Christ takes us up higher in our walk with Him. When going through for His namesake we are blessed.

Sometimes there are things within us that must be removed so there can be a greater move of the anointing in our lives. Sometimes we get inpatient, but I say unto you and myself wait on the Lord. While we wait let us allow the master potter to work on us. *"And the vessel that he made of clay was marred in the hand of the potter: so he made it again another vessel, as seemed good to the potter to make it… Oh house of Israel, cannot I do with you as this potter? Saith the Lord. Behold, as the clay is in the potter's hand, so are ye in mine hand."* (Jeremiah 8:4-6 KJV). While waiting the master potter is bringing forth his glory out of us. In the waiting we are getting more power, joy, strength, and anointing. *"He that believeth on me, the works that I do shall he do also: and greater works than these shall he do."* (John 14:12 KJV). This waiting period is releasing you more in Christ.

There are times we must be silent as we wait. We can get busy doing other things, but God desires silent times as well. Silent times are necessary to hear what the Spirit is saying to us. While waiting there are times the Lord is releasing some things in, out and through us. In the book, Lord of the Impossible: By: Lloyd John Ogilvie. One passage states "An in-depth, comprehensive study of how God called and equipped people to do what they could not do alone reveals the power available to us today." The Lord constantly wants to surprise us with what He can do if we dare to risk, to accept his gift of faith, and to leave the results to him." So I believe what Mr. Ogilvie is saying believe, while you are waiting believe the Lord is going to perform that release you are waiting on.

*"God is not a man, that He should lie; neither the son of man, that He should repent: hath He said, and shall He not do it? Or hath He spoken, and shall He not make it good?"*
(Numbers 23:19 KJV).
We are not waiting on our Heavenly Father in vain. When you are in waiting mode, the enemy which is the devil brings all kinds of attractions to get you frustrated with God. Asking questions like,

Lord how long? Have not I been in this long enough? God's time is not our time, and our time is not God's time always. *"Do all things without murmuring and disputing."* (Philippians 2:14 KJV).

We do not want to be like the children of Israel, but we want to see the promise land of these test. We have been positioned for purpose. God is purposeful in all He does, He appoints us to carry out his mission in earth. God is observing us, his children, to carry out his commission. It is important to Him that we know how to conduct ourselves. This is why we must hold on, stay playful, and wait on God.

We must let God be God in our lives. Yes, sometimes things in our lives get pretty rough. Some things can be a tragedy and break us all the way down, but I have found in those times of testing, reading the promises of God to me (us) in the word of God, picks me up in my spirit man, and I am able to go on in God. I am not going to say waiting always feels good, but knowing that your waiting is ordained of God, and not of ourselves make all the difference.

Remember when you are going through and waiting for the cause of Christ at your lowest point, He steps right in on time. Remember Joseph, Jacob's son, in Genesis Chapter 34 through Chapter 50. Joseph went through a many of things. His brothers wanted to kill him, but by God being in Joseph's life, his brother Reuben came to his rescue. "Let's not kill him", he said. (Genesis 37:21 NLT). They tore his coat of many colors and threw him in a pit, but God had plans for Joseph, just as he has them for us. *"Let's sell Joseph to those Ishmaelite traders, let's not be responsible for his death."* (Genesis 37:26-27 NLT). He was sold to Potiphar, but began to be captain of the Egyptian officer's entire household. But as the enemy would have it Potiphar's wife wanted Joseph for herself, and when he would not sin with her, she lied on him. This encounter sent him to jail. *"Whose feet they hurt with fetters: he was laid in iron."* (Psalm.105:18 KJV). God used these experiences of Joseph to make him strong in Him.

We need to learn, how not to find Christ in our circumstance of waiting. We need to bring him to our circumstance by praying and waiting. My Overseer, Bishop J. J. Woods often tells me, if you can't think of anything to say in your circumstances, that you are in, just say Praise the Lord. It works for me. Yes, waiting can be hard and frustrating. However stop and think, ask yourself this question, have I asked the Lord to teach me how to wait? Believe it once you do, it will become easier. Give God yourself, emotions, mind, and will. Let the Lord began to empower you with his will.

Remember let God be God in your wait. *"Now unto him that is able to keep you from falling, and to present you faultless before the presence of his glory with exceeding joy. To the only wise God our Saviour, be glory and majesty, dominion and power, both now and ever."*(Jude 24-25 KJV).

## About The Author

Bishop Linda Harrison

*Bishop Linda Harrison is the Pastor of From Glory To Glory Apostolic Church Of Church, Located 1487 N. Union Boulevard St. Louis Missouri. E-mail Address: linda8548@sbcglobal.net Bishop Linda Harrison's new life with Christ began May 1980. Bishop Harrison was ordained Missionary in 1982. During that time the Lord began to blessing in her walk with him. In 1993 Bishop Harrison received Ministerial Credential, from W.A. F. World Apostolic Fellowship Inc. East St. Louis IL. Licensed Evangelist and also received National Evangelist and Minister's ordination license. She was chosen Director of U.C.C.C. United Council of Christian Churches, by Presiding Bishop John E. Sheriff of Los Angeles California in 1994. Bishop Harrison was ordained Pastor by Bishop J.J. Woods in 1996. Bishop J.J. Woods also ordained her Bishop in 2001. The Lord has blessed Bishop Linda Harrison to pastor three churches during her ministry in the field of leadership. Many souls have been saved, and she's thanks Jesus Christ for many, many more through this anointed ministry that the Lord has entrusted in her.*

# Chapter 3

## Patience Brings Forth The Promise

*Patience is the companion of wisdom – St. Augustine*

Patience is the fourth fruit of the Spirit and needs to be cultivated and properly tended to with faith, endurance, long suffering and perseverance. *"But the fruit of the Spirit is love, joy, peace, longsuffering, gentleness, goodness, faith. Meekness, temperance: against such there is no law."* (Galatians 5:22-23 KJV). How does this cultivating happen? It takes place through the trials and tests that you experience in your everyday life. It helps to bring you to the place of perfection. *"That the trial of your faith, being much more precious than of gold that perisheth, though it be tried with fire, might be found unto praise and honor and glory at the appearing of the Jesus Christ. Whom having not seen, ye love,; in whom though now ye see him not, yet believing, ye rejoice with joy unspeakable and full of glory; Receiving the end of your faith, even the salvation of your souls."* (1 Peter 1:7-9 KJV). This text speaks in terms of how the heat of trials, struggles, and persecutions will teach you patience and strengthen your faith.

As you look around in today's society you can clearly see that patience is a very rare virtue. It has been called the greatest of all virtues. Wherever you go these days you'll encounter people who are in such a hurry, they don't want to wait, or yield the right of way. Patience is a very challenging fruit to grow in today's fast paced world. It takes time for patience to grow in your life. Let patience have her perfect work. You have to put forth a purposeful effort.

People are extremely impatient, and honestly speaking, we all can lose our patience from time to time and may even find our patience being tested in some way every day. Have you become frustrated waiting for God to answer your prayers, to hear your faintest cry, and give you that breakthrough that you so desperately need? *"We must never get tired of doing good because if we don't give up the struggle we shall get our harvest in proper time."* (Galatians 6:9 Jerusalem Bible). Keep looking up to Jesus. *"Looking unto Jesus the author and finisher of our faith; who for the joy that was set before him endured the cross, despising the shame, and is set down at the right hand of the throne of God."* (Hebrews 12:2 KJV). Be vigilant, mediate on His Word, and pray. If you don't you'll find yourself shifting from trusting God to being consumed with the cares of the world.

In Matthew 14:22-33, Peter walked on the water until he took his eyes off Jesus and felt the forces around him and he began sink, but he was smart enough to cry out "Lord help me" and immediately Jesus helped him. Do you feel like you are sinking and crying out Lord, Help me? "God is our refuge and strength, a very present help in trouble."(Psalm 46:1 KJV). Even the seasoned saint can be subject to faint and become overwhelmed when troubles come and life throws a curb ball; your heart and flesh can fail. Jeremiah said *"Thus saith the LORD; cursed be the man that trusteth in man, and maketh flesh his arm, and whose heart departeth from the Lord."* (Jeremiah 17:5 KJV). We have to remain faithful and. someone may say how do I keep from fainting while waiting for the promises of God? King David penned one of the answers *"I had fainted, unless I had believed to see the goodness of the Lord in the land of the living. Wait on the Lord: be of good courage, and he shall strengthen thine heart: wait, I say, on the Lord."*(Psalm 27:13-14 KJV).

    Precious ones believe that the Lord will help you to make it in due time and that you will outlive your troubles and tests. Trust that God is working in your situation. Keep the promises of God before you. What has the Lord promised you? Just begin to rehearse the promises of the Lord. Keep confessing them say them out loud again and again.

*"Yes the rain and the snow come down from the heavens an do not return without watering the earth, making it yield and giving growth to provide seed for sower and bread for the eating, so the word that goes out from my mouth does not return to me empty, without carrying out my will and succeeding in what was sent to do."*(Isaiah 55:10-11 Jerusalem Bible). *"He gives strength to the wearied, he strengthens the powerless. Young men may grow tired and weary, youths may stumble, but those who hope in Yahweh renew their strength, they put out wings like eagles. They run and do not grow weary, walk and never tire."*(Isaiah 40:29-31 Jerusalem Bible). The provisions of God are in His promise. *"But seek first the kingdom of God, and his righteousness; and all these things shall be added unto you. Take no thought for the morrow: for the morrow shall take thought for the things of itself. Sufficient unto the day is the evil thereof."*
(Matthew 6: 33-34 KJV).

    Our heavenly father has given us so many powerful promises; salvation, joy, peace, prosperity healing, safety, deliverance, and so much more. The dictionary defines promise as 1.) A vow; 2.) Pledge something; 3.) Make somebody expect something; 4) Assurance or undertaking; and 5.) Indication of success. *"For all the promises of God in him are yea, and in him amen unto the glory of God by us."*(II Corinthians 1:20 KJV). You have to believe that they will come to pass. Jesus said in the Book of Mark, *"For verily I say unto you, that whosoever shall say unto this mountain, be thou removed, and cast into the sea: and shall not doubt in his heart, but shall believe that those things which He saith shall come to pass; he shall have whatsoever He saith. Therefore I say unto you, what things so ever ye desire, when ye pray believe that ye receive them, and ye shall have them."*(Mark 11:23-24 KJV).

These promises are available to us through faith. When I think about what it means to have patience while waiting on God to do what he has promised, Genesis 15, 16 & 21, Romans 4:16- 21 comes to mind. These scriptures remind us of the consequences that Abraham, Sarah and the world experienced because of not trusting in the timing of God. They choose to use Hagar as the first surrogate and produced Ishmael (the flesh) (Genesis 16:16 KJV) because they would not wait on the promise (Isaac). (Genesis 21: 2 KJV). There is a price to pay for disobedience. "The blessings of Yahweh is what brings riches, to this hard toil has nothing to add."(Proverbs 10:22 NJV). God never promised us anything that He could not deliver. If we only believe that with faith all things are possible and without it nothing is possible. Faith fulfills the promises of God. Walk in the counsel and wisdom of God so you will not fall into the trap of the enemy and allow doubt, fear, and unbelief to enter into your being. *"But without faith it is impossible to please him; for he that cometh to God must believe that he is, and that he is a rewarder of them that diligently seek him."*(Hebrews 11:6 KJV). While a measure of faith has been given to every person exercise yours. *"For I say, through the grace given unto me, to every man that is among you, not to think of himself more highly than he ought to think; but to think soberly, according as God hath dealt to every man the measure of faith."*(Romans 12:3 KJV). What is faith? It's pistis in the Greek meaning: a firm persuasion, being fully convinced about who God is. *"Now faith is the substance of things hoped the evidence of things not seen."*(Hebrews 11:1 KJV).

*"So then faith cometh by hearing, and hearing by the word of God."*(Romans 10:17 KJV). Walking with God requires that you

hear from Him. Listen and obey Him. People have faith in a lot of things, but I am talking about having faith in God and believing that God will do exactly what He says he will do. *"God is not a man that he should lie; neither the son of man, that he should repent: hath he said, and shall he not do it? or hath he spoken, and shall he not make it good?"*(Numbers 23:19 KJV). *"Therefore it is of faith, that it might be by grace, to the end the promise might be sure to all the seed; not to that only which is of the law, but to that also which is of the faith of Abraham; who is the father of us All. As it is written, I have made thee a father of many nations before whom he believed, and God, who quickeneth the dead, and calleth those things which be not as though they were. Who against hope believed in hope that he might become the father of many nations, according to that which was spoken, so shall thy seed be. And being not weak in faith, he considered not his own body now dead, when he was an hundred years old, neither yet the deadness of Sarah's womb. He staggered not at the promise of God through unbelief; but was strong in faith, giving glory to God. And being fully persuaded that, what he had promised, he was able also to perform."*(Romans 4:16-21 KJV).

    In the text God promised Abraham and Sarah a son. They had to wait a quarter of a century for the fulfillment of that promise. How long have you been waiting for your promise? As we study the scriptures we learn that there is a relationship between faith, hope and patience. Troubles will come to prove how authentic your faith is, and to try and test the purity of your faith, which is so precious and worth more than gold that perishes. Abraham was a man who certainly possessed the virtue of patience. He remains an example of what it truly means to exercise strong faith while waiting on the Lord to do what He has promised.

    We are instructed in (Isaiah 51:2) to look to him. May we follow his example and staggered not at the promises of God. The Bible teaches that pain, adversity, and temptation are involved in patience. Are you ready for your promise?

When you read scriptures like *"My brethren, count it all joy when you fall into divers temptations; Knowing this, that the trying of your faith worketh patience. But let patience have her perfect work, that you may be perfect and entire, wanting nothing."* (James 1:2-4 KJV). *"And not so, but we glory in tribulations also: knowing that tribulations worketh patience; And patience, experience: and experience hope."* (Romans 5:3-4 KJV). These scriptures speak of how difficulties help you grow and teach how to rejoice in the times of suffering. We recognize that God will use difficulties to build our character, strengthen our faith and give us hope. "Patience is the willingness to wait on the promises of God with the expectancy of assured faith." – Kimus Bouknight.

*"For all the promises of God in him are yea, and in him amen unto the glory of God by us."* (I Corinthians 1:20 KJV). You have to believe that they will come to pass. Jesus said in Mark *"For verily I say unto you, that whosoever shall say unto this mountain, be thou removed, and cast into the sea: and shall not doubt in his heart, but shall believe that those things which he saith shall come to pass; he shall have whatsoever he saith. Therefore I say unto you, what things so ever ye desire, when ye pray believe that ye receive them, and ye shall have them."* (Mark 11:23-24).

As you wait for the promise of God, "Go the Distance." Jesus went the distance. He was the seed of the woman promised. *"And I will put enmity between thee and the woman, and between thy seed and her seed; it shall bruise thy head, and thou shalt bruise his heel."* (Genesis 3:15 KJV). He was proclaimed by the prophets of Israel to be the Lamb of God and the Savior of the world.

He was born in a cattle stall. As a Jew, the Son of Man was born into an atmosphere of racial hatred. He was born into the political oppression of the Roman government, whose brutality stained the soil of the nations in rivers of innocent blood. The legitimacy of Christ's birth was in question from His first breath.

When He began His ministry, the recognized spiritual

leaders called Him a heretic. Mary saw Him as an infant in Bethlehem's manger. John the Baptist saw Him as a candidate for water baptism. The disciples saw Him as their Jewish Rabbi. The Roman government considered Him an insurrectionist too dangerous to live and executed Him with brutality known as the crucifixion at the place called Calvary. His provision came on the cross, when he shouted, *"It is finished!"* What was finished? Sin was finished, for, *"If the Son therefore shall make you free, ye shall be free indeed."*(John 8:36 KJV).

The right attitude can help you get the victory. While you are waiting for patience to produce the promise I say rejoice. *"His anger lasts a moment, his favour a lifetime; in the evening, a spell of tears, in the morning, shouts of joy."*(Psalm 30:5 Jerusalem Bible). "For ye have need of patience that after you have done the will of God, ye might receive the promise."(Hebrews 10:36 KJV). *"I am Alpha and O'me-ga, the beginning and the ending, saith the Lord, which is, and which was, and which is to come, the Almighty."*(Revelation 1:8 KJV).

### *Prayer*

*Father, Thank you for this project, the Women Of God Ministries and for souls that this book touches help us to live in your counsel and wisdom daily, as we renew our minds through your word and develop the fruit of patience in our lives. Thank you for the change in us in Jesus Name Amen.*

*So many cries, so many pleas, so many "Lord Have Mercy", so many "Father I Stretch My Hand to Thee", those that cry "Pass Me Not", "Help Me Lord Jesus", "Lord Forgive me" and "Draw Me Nearer". Yes, so many, on and on and on.*
AND HE STILL HEARS
*The faintest cry*
*The lowest sigh.*
*The weakest moan*
*The painful groan.*
*The soft spoken*
*The heart broken*
*The muted one*
*The imprisoned con*
*The loud mouthed*
*The shattered.*
*The depressed*
*The oppressed*
*The flashy one*
*The raggedy one*
Yet He Still Hears
Yet, "*your father knows the things you have need of before you ask Him*"
Georgia Woolridge, June 2010

## About The Author

Evangelist Lisa Renee' Johnson-Bouknight
Elect Lady

Evangelist Lisa Renee' Bouknight, is one of God's chosen and anointed vessels and she ministers as a teacher, and preacher. She is a committed member of the Second Refreshing Spring COGIC in Washington, DC. She serves there as the president of the women's department, Sunday school teacher for the adult class. She is married to Pastor Kimus J. Bouknight and together they have seven children and eleven grandchildren. Evangelist Bouknight surrendered her life to the Lord in 1980 under the leadership of Bishop Frank White Sr. of Mt. Zion COGIC, Freeport, New York during a watch night service. She was licensed as Evangelist/Minister in May of 1991 by the late Pastor James Staggers, New Tabernacle Baptist Church, Bronx, New York. Lisa also received an Evangelist license under the leadership of Pastor James E. Jordan Jr. Refreshing Spring COGIC, Riverdale, Maryland. She is a graduate of New York Theological Seminary, Queens Broadcasting School and Refreshing Spring Bible College. She has traveled the country ministering in revivals, workshop, seminars, and conferences, and has done extensive prison ministry. She is a member of the State Evangelist Jurisdictional District of Washington, DC, the A.D. Headen District Sunday school field representative, Instructor for the Jurisdictional Educational Department, and Pastor's Wives Circle. Lisa is implementing Arise Daughters of Zion Ministries, Inc. Her life is a testimony of the grace and mercy of almighty God. She has completely surrendered and committed her life and ministry into the hands of Almighty God.

# Chapter 4

## *Does He Know?*

God knows everything. He knows it all at one glance. God knows perfectly and He knows it all at once. He does not grow more intelligent with time. God does not gain or lose knowledge. He cannot grow wiser. He has perfect knowledge. He has had perfect knowledge of everything knowable throughout eternity. -Richard "Dick" Hill.

God is omniscient. The Merriam-Webster dictionary defines omniscient as having infinite awareness, understanding and insight; possessed of universal or complete knowledge. As God's creation we must understand the attributes of Gods infinite wisdom. *"The eyes of the Lord are in every place, beholding the evil and the good."*(Proverbs 15:3 KJV). As stated in the scripture God's eyes see everything. What a powerful God, to be able see every intricate detail of his creation. *"Shall not God search this out? For he knoweth the secrets of the heart."*(Psalm 44:21 KJV). There is no secret that can be hidden from God. That is why it is imperative that we are transparent when communing with God. He knows everything anyway.

As we face trials and tribulations many times we feel the anguish and pain of our circumstances. Then we begin to focus on the situations and they begin to magnify. We sometimes lose focus that God even exists. Worry, depression, disappointment, frustration, hurt, confusion can cloud our perspective. What do we do when faced with such dilemmas? In order, to survive We must remember who God is and who we are in God, in order to survive. Application of God's word is one of the most important components in our walk with God. Allowing the word to become manifested in our lives sustains us through hard times. Why? Because God is his Word.

God used great men and women throughout the Bible as instruments to exemplify how one can be sustained through adversity as they obeyed his word. We have a responsibility to follow the precepts of God. When we obey His word and govern our lives by His word then anything we pray in His name will come to pass. When we ask amiss for things we will not receive the blessing. That is why it important that we make sure what we are asking for is in alignment with his word. If not we will face disappointment and think that God does not know. There are decisions that we make that will make it seem like God is not there. We must realize that we cannot manipulate God. People who try to manipulate God often become rebellious. They say "He does not know". Rebellious people are full of pride and have a mindset that they are smarter than God.

God is a God of Foreknowledge meaning He knows all things before they happen. I remember about nineteen years ago while sitting in The Church Of The Redeemed Of The Lord, I kept having visions of my father lying in a casket. I did not understand why I kept seeing that image. Being troubled and perplexed I went to my Pastor Jerome Stokes Sr. and explained to him what I was seeing. He explained to me that what I was experiencing was the gift of foreknowledge. He directed me to the book of Genesis. *"And the*

*Lord said shall I hide from Abraham that thing which I do."*(Genesis 18:17 KJV). God cared so much for Abraham that he wanted to share with him what was about to take place in Sodom and Gomorrah. Pastor Stokes explained to me how we could walk so close to God that we would obtain favor in his sight.

*"Seeing that Abraham shall surely become a great and mighty nation and all the nations shall be blessed in him? For I know him, that he will command his children and his household after him, and they shall keep the way of the Lord, to do justice and judgment, that the Lord may bring upon Abraham that which he hath spoken of him. And the Lord said, because the cry of Sodom and Gomorrah is great, and because their Sin is very grievous. I will go down now, and see whether they have done altogether according to the cry of it which is come unto me, and if not I will know. And the men turned their faces from thence and went toward Sodom; but Abraham stood up before the Lord."*(Genesis 18:18-22 KJV).

As we can see Abraham had much favor with God. Pastor Stokes also elaborated how we could intercede on behalf of our loved ones that God would grant mercy to them just as Abraham had done. He told me as we read the word; we must know that God's word is real. It is not a fairy tale. I was a babe in Christ at the time, but I still listened to everything the man of God revealed to me. I applied it to my life. Two weeks later my sister came into the church while service was going on and told me that my father had been shot. He was taken to Shock Trauma at University of Maryland Hospital in Baltimore, Maryland. The word that Pastor Stokes directed me to came to mind. The word sustained me and I was able to be strong for my father and family. I went to the hospital and spoke with the doctors. They advised me that because my father had lost a lot of blood, they were unsure if he would make it through the night. I visited briefly, although my father was in an unconscious state. I spoke with Pastor Stokes, who told me he was praying for us. I stayed up the whole night making intercession for my father just like Abraham made intercession for his family. The next morning I went to the hospital and my father was still alive. I truly was rejoicing in the Lord. I really got to see through that experience that God truly knows all things. I thank God for placing a true man of God as my covering, Bishop Jerome Stokes Sr. *"Hast thou not known? Hast thou not heard that the everlasting God, the Lord, the creator of the ends of the earth, fainteth not, neither is weary? There is no searching of his understanding."* (Isaiah 40:28 KJV).

    God's knowledge unlike ours does not come in a series of thoughts, one following the other. The events in time do not parade across God's mind to be viewed event by event. He sees all of history at one glance (Hill).

    As we all know there has been a breakdown in the economic state of man. People are losing jobs, homes, businesses, material possessions. God is not affected by anything traumatic that is going on in society. He never grows weary nor does He get weak when adversity comes. That is why it is important that we seek the face of God like never before in these perilous times. We need his strength and direction because the kingdom of God does not ever suffer lack. These calamities are happening due to the greed and corruption of man. Does God Know? Yes! He knows. He has all of the answers to these problems. Whenever, a nation or man turns away from God they cause oppression to come upon them from the enemy. *"And they said unto him, There came a man up to meet us, and said unto us. Go turn again unto the King that sent you, and say unto him, Thus said the Lord; it is not because there is not a God in Israel that thou sendest to enquire of Baal-zebub the god of Ekron? Therefore thou shalt not come down from that bed on which thou art gone up, but shall surely die."* (II Kings 1:6 KJV). Through God's infinite wisdom He always has raised up men and women of integrity to deliver his people.

    That is why we must not resist suffering. As we suffer in the flesh we are dying to ourselves. One thing we have to realize is that all of the status and the worldly possessions do not validate us. What validates us is the word and ways of God. As we dwell and walk in the wisdom and strength of God he will continue to guide and lead us. Before, a building can be constructed there has to be blueprints for that building. God's word is the blueprints of our construction of our temples of the Holy Ghost. The blueprint of God's word will guide us into places of spiritual prosperity as well as natural prosperity. *"Delight thyself in the Lord, and he shall give thee the desires of thine heart. Commit thy way unto the Lord, and he shall bring it to pass."*(Psalm 37:4-5 KJV). Let us not be a people that want quick satisfaction. Let us wait on the Lord. *"I waited patiently for the Lord, and he inclined unto me, and heard my cry."*(Psalm 40:1 KJV). Whenever I have not waited on God I made a disaster of every situation. It was God's mercy and grace that kept me. Through those experiences I have cried out to God and have asked him to show me the error of my ways. As I honestly evaluated myself and the situations according to the word of God, I could always see my mistakes. When we do not heed the word of God we fall into pitfalls. The word is the wisdom of God which protect and preserve us.

*"My son forget not my law, but let thine heart keep my commandments. For length of days, and long life, and peace shall they add to thee."*(Proverbs 3:1-2 KJV).

*"Then the word of the Lord came unto me, saying, Before I formed thee in the belly I knew thee and before thou camest forth out of the womb I sanctified thee, and I ordained thee a prophet unto the nations."*(Jeremiah 1:4-5 KJV).

Now reading these verses I get excited! The word tells me that before I was even in the womb of my mother God knew me. Wow! He knows His plans for my life. When adversity comes I can draw on His sovereignty. When I feel overwhelmed with the pressures of life I can meditate of this verse and say wait a minute God knew me before He formed me. Therefore, if He knew me then He knows everything that is attempting to overthrow me. I separate myself from the wisdom of this world and I seek Him. He brings me through the test and trials while He brings glory to himself. Then as He delivers me He is making my character to resemble Him more. It is all about us resembling Christ and bringing glory to his name, especially when there are so many false religions that oppose his greatness. We have to defend His honor and His Kingdom principles.

The vastness of Christ serves to allow us to be confident in the fact that He is all knowing. Even with all of these great attributes he still makes intercession for us. *"And he that searcheth the hearts knoweth what is the mind of the Spirit, because he maketh intercession for the saints according to the will of God."* (Romans 8:27 KJV). Now He knows what is going on still because He makes intercession for us. He has not stopped interceding for us. Prayer is a powerful weapon that is used to keep the lines of communication open. It is vitally important that we commune with God continuously. He knows what is of the mind and of the spirit. Almighty God, all powerful and all knowing is also allowing us to have the privilege of prayer. We do not have to go to a man because the veil was rent. Just imagine in your minds, if you were in the military fighting a war and your commanding officer has all of the orders to give you to allow you and your platoon to win the war. Would you stop communicating with him or her? No you would not because you would be afraid to die in the battle. However, God almighty has all knowledge and wisdom in reference to this spiritual battle. Why should we not pray and commune with him in reference to this battle? We must not become weakened by the cares of this life.

God also knows about any emotional hurt or betrayal we may experience. Judas Iscariot is noted in history as the one who betrayed Jesus. His being called with the other disciples is somewhat mysterious. Yet Judas was first numbered among the twelve disciples. *"And when it was day, he called unto him his disciples, and of them he chose twelve, whom also he named apostles."* (Luke

6:13 KJV). "Then entered Satan into Judas surnamed Iscariot, being of the number of the twelve."(Luke 22:3 KJV). *"Men and brethren this scripture must needs have been fulfilled, which the Holy Ghost by the mouth of David spake before concerning Judas, which was guide to them that took, Jesus. For he was numbered with us, and had obtained part of this ministry."*(Acts 1:16-17 KJV). Here it is that Judas who walked so closely with the King Of Kings betrayed him. Judas possessed the same spirit and mind set as Satan. This clearly shows when someone's heart is not right and they are given power, it only amplifies what is wrong, not what is right. Clearly his heart was not in the right place. Even the hurt and betrayal that we have and may experience conditions us to still walk in love. It does not mean that when we walk in love with people that hurt us that they will ever repent. The important thing is that we do not violate any of God's commandments. We as a people must realize that offences will come but, they are sent to try to hinder us. As we see Christ's example He just kept showing Judas love and kept His focus. We can never be deceived into thinking that we will not experience emotional pain and hurt, as well as betrayal. It is clear that this is another tactic that Satan uses to try to overthrow us. As we fast, pray and walk in love, God will even protect us as we go through these experiences. He is acquainted with our sufferings. We must recognize as we submit to God, his omniscience protects us from all things that will attempt to hinder and destroy us.

## About The Author

### Charity Hope Jones

*Elder Charity Hope Jones serves on the Ministerial Staff at Church Of The Redeemed Of Lord. under the leadership of Bishop Jerome Stokes, where she has been a member for twenty-one years. She has served in many capacities such as the Sound Media, Outreach Ministry and Community Support Center, as well as leading the Intercessory Prayer Team. She has travelled and ministered in several states teaching on topics such as prayer, marriage, dating, single and saved, generational curses, and spiritual warfare just to name a few. She has also served as a part-time Assistant Pastor at God's Church Of Grace & Mercy. Being a servant of the Lord, Elder Jones enjoys visiting and ministering to God's people in hospitals and prisons. She currently oversees the Fresh Dew Prayer Intercessory Ministry affiliated with Women Of God Ministries. Elder Jones also assists with The "Clarion Call" under the Direction of Pastor Trena Stephenson and is delighted to witness many people delivered and set free from the yokes of bondage. Using her degree in Business Administration, Elder Jones desires to further utilize her God given gifts to set up programs for women, men and children. Elder Jones has committed her life to empowering and ministering to the whole person; and seeing families restored and set free. Elder Jones believes as a servant of the most High God it is her responsibility to serve God's people, love, protect and cover them in prayer.*

# Chapter 5

*Does He Care?*
*"The Power of Empathy"*

There are many instances when we as human beings have asked the question: Does God still care? This question is typically asked when we experience unexpected moments in life. Issues like broken relationships, death, disappointment, abuse, neglect, injury and any other emotional violating circumstance of reality, we usually try to subconsciously ignore. These issues tend to usher us to as the age old question: Does God still care? Issues like these we usually try to subconsciously ignore that tend to ushers us to ask this age old question. In actuality, we eventually have to acknowledge and respect the unpredictability's of life and its irregularities.

Through our life experiences, difficult times usually stir up our emotions leaving our hearts unsettled causing us to feel isolated as if we are the only one having that experience. In isolated moments, as expected, our minds start to wonder, attempting to put that event in spiritual perspective leading us to ask the question: Does God still care?

We tend to try to make pain and suffering parallel with the notion or concept that God is answering that question for us. This causes us to misinterpret things or events that are inevitable. For example, experiencing the death of a close love one can cause one to misunderstand the experience as a representation of how God feels about them. This is simply not the case. The greatest advice that I could give from my own experiences is to pray. Pray that God can help you see how He still cares in the mist of distress. God knows and feels every single human emotion that you could ever feel. Not only because He is the author of those emotions, but because we are made in His image. We are actually experiencing His emotions. Fortunately, as a result of my prayers, God has allowed me to meet people who have experienced similar things in life as I have experienced. He used my testimonies to give others hope.

As humans, we are naturally more in tuned with the emotions and experiences of others that mirror our own. This can be a positive and also a negative because it highlights the functional differences between sympathy and empathy.

Does God have that option? Can He be either sympathetic or empathetic? The answer to these questions is NO. God is concerned about His people. He doesn't waiver back and forth from sympathetic to empathetic, He is consistently empathic. Not only is God empathic towards our distresses, He put Himself in our shoes. He experienced life as a human being to test the realities of life, death, betrayal, abuse, disappointment etc. Does God care? Yes. Furthermore, God is concerned whether His children care for others as He cares for us. For example, we may think: "Of course God loves the poor; he loves everybody." Except it's not as simple as that; God's character is presented as a model for our own. If God values the poor, we have to think about what that means for us.

As Christians, we should seek to cultivate this one of many beautiful attributes of God. Our goal should be to learn how to use the power of empathy towards every human being. We should exhibit empathy regardless of race, gender, social or cultural status, sexual preference, title, denomination or whatever category that society conforms our thoughts to use as a natural human divider.

Is there an elephant in the room? It seems as if we are afraid to acknowledge that there is some sort of fear that is preventing us from extending ourselves to others. Fears that can leave us emotionally, physically or spiritually exploited which creates calluses on the heart. Well, you may ask, what is a callus? A callus is thickened skin that appears on the feet or hands which develops in response to pressure. They are actually a normal and natural way for the body to protect itself. For example, callus develops on the hand when chopping a lot of wood. It's a normal way for the skin to protect itself. The problem occurs when the pressure continues, so the skin gets thicker. It eventually becomes painful and is treated as something foreign by the body. In a spiritual context, a callused heart is a thickened layer on the heart that prevents us from embracing the empathetic characteristics of God. It's develops in response to pressures of life experiences, disappointments, hurts, anxieties, burdens, and hassles eventually resulting into unbearable experiences. Soon after, our ability to care for others is viewed as something foreign to us.

We must remember that God created us out of love, in love and to love. Scripture communicates to us in I Corinthians 13:13 that the greatest of faith, hope and love is love. *"If someone says, I love God, and hates his brother, he is a liar; for he who does not love his brother whom he has seen, how can he love God whom he has not seen?"* (I John 4:20 New King James Version NKJV). It is baffling to witness so many Christians quoting biblical text while ignoring the spiritual and social injustices that happen in any community. Not only does God care and is empathic towards you and your individual circumstances, He cares about everybody's. We already know that God cares about us, but do we care about God enough to move beyond our own level of comfort to show others through our actions that God cares about them. *"You shall do no injustice in judgment. You shall not be partial to the poor, nor honor the person of the mighty. In righteousness you shall judge your neighbor. You shall not go about as a talebearer among your people; nor shall you take a stand against the life of your neighbor: I am the LORD. You shall not hate your brother in your heart. You shall surely rebuke your neighbor, and not bear sin because of him. You shall not take vengeance, nor bear any grudge against the children of your people, but you shall love your neighbor as yourself: I am the LORD."*(Leviticus 19:15-18 NKJV).

      Hate is the adversary that wages war against empathy. It is a very strong word. However, according to Merriam-Webster Thesaurus , there are other words that camouflage it such as disgust and dislike. Which one of these words inhibits you from extending empathy in your actions? What we need to realize is that sometimes God can reveal Himself through our behaviors, one of which is listening. Hate, disgust or dislike creates a spiritual deaf ear however, empathy involves listening. A kind of listening that is not judgmental, defensive, critical or suspicious. How would we feel if every approach that God made to listen to our prayers was judgmental, defensive, critical or suspicious? We would not like it, in fact, we all subconsciously expect God to show us a certain level of empathy. Even if you feel disdained or defeated, God expects us to take care of one another. Cain asked, *"Am I my brother's keeper?"*(Genesis 4:9 NKJV). It seems as if we always ask the questions we already know the answer to rather than asking the questions to the ones we don't. If you don't know the answer ask God in prayer, and He cares enough to answer.

      Even in the mist of our pain we have to pull on God, prayer and the positive people that He has placed in our lives to help us to push through our emotions to extend ourselves to others. Jesus is a perfect example. Before his crucifixion, He prayed to God throughout agony, push through His emotions, pulling on the essence of empathy and love. He was able to care enough to sacrifice Himself our sins. It is essential that we challenge ourselves and others to practice being more empathetic to one another. It is vital that we as humans practice tenderness with one another. It is critical that we challenge ourselves and others practice godliness toward one another. We are to conform ourselves to godliness by practicing the deeds and following in the footsteps of Jesus Christ.

The power of empathy proves to the world that God still cares. It can defeat and conquer all spiritual and social injustices. It can devour what others assume are incidental inequalities. The concept of empathy is distinct and can be practiced by any human being. It's a moral and ethical practice that communities and society has eased from its responsibility. Empathy, love and care supersede anything that lies dormant in the hearts of humans. We just have to open our minds and embrace it in our hearts so that we can demonstrate, illustrate and prove to others through our actions that God does care.

## About The Author

### Rev. Brandi W. Blocker

*Rev. Brandi W. Blocker was born and raised in New Orleans, Louisiana. She is a deacon in the African Methodist Episcopal Church and a member of St. Stephens AME Church located in Essex, Maryland. Brandi is also the Marketing and Public Relations Director of Daughters of Distinction. She is a graduate of Dillard University (New Orleans, Louisiana) with a Bachelor of Arts degree in Business, a graduate of University of Findlay (Toledo, Ohio) with a Masters in Business Administration and Public Administration. She is presently a student at Payne Theological Seminary in Wilberforce, Ohio graduating with a Masters in Divinity May 2011. She is married, has two children and currently resides in Baltimore, Maryland.*

# Chapter 6

*What's In Your Heart?*

Deuteronomy 6:5 *"Love the LORD your God with all your heart and with all your soul and with all your strength"* (New International Version NIV).

According to Strong's Hebrew Dictionary , the Hebrew word for heart is "lebab." The definition means inner man, mind, will, heart, soul, understanding, knowledge, thinking, reflection, memory; of moral character. To love God with all the heart, and with all the understanding, we must know Him.

What is in my heart is to know Him and to know Him requires intimacy with Him! Intimacy is marked by close acquaintance, association or familiarity; a quiet atmosphere; detailed knowledge; private utterance or action; sexual act; familiarity; understanding; confidence.

Picture sitting on a carpet of the softest, greenest grass you have ever seen under a crystal blue sky as the warm sun glistens on the lake in front of you. The water is so clear you could practically see your reflection. The weather is perfectly warm with a very soft breeze flowing through the trees. The trees are dancing to the songs of the birds chirping in the background. The two of us completely focused on each other and engaged in the most interesting conversation ever! There is no other place I would rather be than in the presence of my Father! The Father and me! Some might say this is heaven! I say it is heaven on earth! I call this intimacy at its highest level. It is a place where the Father and I meet alone. Nothing else matters! No interruptions! He has my full attention and I have His! Intimacy with the Father! Yes, into me see! See into my heart Lord!

Intimacy is about getting as close as you can to a person while getting to know them. It is a close relationship that involves vulnerability and transparency. Intimacy happens in quiet atmospheres, sometimes intimacy is a private utterance or action between two people. It is closeness, a familiarity, an understanding of having confidence in a person and willing to share detailed information about each other. There are different kinds of intimacy - intimacy with our children, parents or friends or between a husband and wife. However intimacy with my Father is the best!

*"As the deer pants (long for) for streams of water, so my soul (mind, will, emotions) pants for you, O God. My soul thirsts for God, for the living God. When can I go and meet with God?"*(Psalm 42:1-2 NIV). The deer, an animal which is naturally hot and dry, longs for streams of water. If the deer does not get water, it will die. Finding water is a priority for the deer. It is a matter of life and death! The psalmist describes the deer as not just "thirsting" no; the deer is "panting." Panting denotes another level of thirst. Panting conjures up an image of immediate need – something that is required to sustain life. The deer pants for streams of water. Why "streams of water?" The stream is constant and never runs dry. Just like the Holy Spirit, constant and never runs dry.

*O God, you are my God, earnestly I seek you; my soul thirsts for you, my body longs for you, in a dry and weary land where there is no water."*(Psalm 63:1 NIV). One of the most powerful natural appetites is the craving for water. My soul thirsts for Him! Everything inside of us should thirst for God! Our mind, will, and emotions need God's direction. Besides its natural significance, "thirst" is figuratively used as a strong spiritual desire. We should want more of God! Panting for Him! Thirsting for Him! We should no longer be satisfied with waiting until we get to Heaven. We should want to know Him while we are here on earth! My heart aches and longs to be with Him. I am heart sick because I need more of Him! *"Blessed are those who hunger and thirst for righteousness, for they will be filled."*(Matthew 5:6 NIV). The soul thirsts for God. Jesus meets the soul's thirst with water of life. *"I am the bread of life. He who comes to me will never go hungry, and he who believes in me will never be thirsty."*(John 6:35-NIV). *"On the last and greatest day of the Feast, Jesus stood and said in a loud voice, If anyone is thirsty, let him come to me and drink."*(John 7:37-NIV). It is said of the heavenly bliss, "Never again will they hunger; never again will they thirst."(Revelation 7:16-NIV).

We too are panting. My soul pants for you O God! Are you panting for God? So when will you go and meet with Him? Is it after you have exhausted all your resources? Is after you have done all "you" can do? Are you willing to meet with Him early in the morning? God is waiting for us to open our heart and tell Him what is in our heart. *"O God, You are my God; Early will I seek* (shacar – to look for diligently) *You; My soul* (nephesh – heart hungers) *thirsts for You; My flesh longs for You In a dry* (tsiyah – wilderness) *and thirsty land where there is no water."*(Psalm 63:1 NKJV).

God longs for us to seek Him! Why early in the morning? Early is necessary because it is before the usual or expected time. It is when the atmosphere is quiet, before your day gets started. Everything inside of us should hunger and thirst for God in a dry place where there is no water (life). We need God to search us, examine us thoroughly to tell us what is really in our heart, on our minds. *"O LORD, you have searched* (examined) *me and known me. You know sitting and my rising up; you understand my thought* (purpose) *afar off. You comprehend my path and my lying down; you are acquainted with all my ways."* (Psalm 139:1-3 NKJV).

We know there no good thing in our heart. Why is it important for God to search us? It is important for God to search us because He knows us! Strong's Hebrew definition for "yada" is to know in a relational sense; to recognize and to be acquainted with; to know by experience; or to have knowledge of someone. God created us in His likeness and image. He knows us but do we know Him?

On this journey to get to know God, God revealed to me the different levels that our relationship goes through with Him. Here are the "Five Levels of Intimacy.

**Level I – The Invitation: Come**

The first level of intimacy is the easiest and most superficial. God is inviting us to come and enjoy an engaged, relaxed, personal and conversational relationship with Him. On this level, we are excited about our salvation. This is the level where I wanted everybody to know I was saved. I was on fire for God! I did everything the word said but it was a surfaced relationship. There was no substance to the relationship. When the tests came my way, the real me came out. Oh, I could quote some scriptures and I thought I had this salvation thing conquered. However when I became irritated, mistreated or offended, I forgot all about the scriptures and God. Early in relationships, we are sometimes trying to determine if the relationship is a "love thing" or are we just "kicking it." "Kicking it" means hanging out for fun with no real purpose. At this level of intimacy, I knew in my heart something was missing and I did not know what it was but God knew. So God invited me to come to Him and drink (John 7:37 NIV). I did not know how to handle this relationship because it was new and different. God heard my heart even when I did not know how to articulate what was in it. *"Search me, O God, and know my heart; test me and know my anxious thoughts"*(Psalm 139:23 24 NIV).

## Level II – Infatuation: It's Only Temporary

Once I achieved this level, I knew in my heart I loved God. My passion was intense but temporary and sometimes irrational. *"I love you, O LORD, my strength"* (Psalm 18:1 NIV). During this level, I only saw God for what He could do for me. I did not see Him for who was because of my selfishness. In other words, I only spent time with God when it benefited me. If the relationship was not going to benefit me then I was no longer interested. This is very painful for me to admit because I know it hurt God. I don't think any of us want someone to be with us only if it benefits them. It doesn't feel good when a relationship is one-sided. I could only love Him based on what I knew about Him, which wasn't much. I knew God loved me but my love for Him was predicated on my feelings and emotions instead of worshipping Him. My love for Him was only temporary.

## Level III – The Middle: The Good, the Bad, the Ugly

This level is really interesting! This level is where the stripping begins. This can be a painful experience because God really begins to take us on a journey to test what is in our heart. This is not a time to be rebellious, this is a time to listen and be obedient. *"Do not harden your hearts as you did at Meribah [ ] as you did that day at Massah[ ] in the desert, where your fathers tested and tried me, though they had seen what I did. For forty years I was angry with that generation; I said, They are a people whose hearts go astray, and they have not known my ways."*(Psalm 95:8-10 NIV). Meribah is known as a place of testing and a place of arguing. Massah is Hebrew for "journey." It was the term used in the Torah to denote the life-changing journey the people of Israel made into the land of Israel. Massah provides a unique experience for young adult Jewish believers in Jesus who desired a deeper relationship with God, a stronger sense of identity. *"If someone claims, He who says, I know Him, and does not keep His commandments, is a liar, and the truth is not in him. But whoever keeps His word, truly the love of God is perfected in him. By this we know that we are in Him. He who says he abides in Him ought himself also to walk just as He walked."* (1 John 2:4-6 NKJV).

**Level IV – The Crossroads: Choose Life or Death/Blessings or Curses**

*"This day I call heaven and earth as witnesses against you that I have set before you life and death, blessings and curses. Now choose life, so that you and your children may live and that you may love the LORD your God, listen to his voice, and hold fast to him. For the LORD is your life, and he will give you many years in the land he swore to give to your fathers, Abraham, Isaac and Jacob."* (Deuteronomy 30:19-20 NIV). This level is where we have to make some decisions. We are sitting at the crossroads and need to decide whether or not we are with God. Do we want life or death, blessings or curses? Once I reached this level, I realized my life was no longer my own. It now belonged to God and I had to decide if I was going to choose to live, not just for me but for my children so they may live. This level teaches us that this journey is not just about ourselves. Our life, our decisions impact others!

**Level V – Maturity: Increase My Faith**

As we move to level V, our relationship with God has gone from being babes and immature to becoming seasoned mature Christians. We have been walking with God for quite some time and even though we are being tested in many areas in our life, we have learned to trust in God with all our heart. *"Consider it pure joy, my brothers, whenever you face trials of many kinds, because you know that the testing of your faith develops perseverance. Perseverance must finish its work so that you may be mature and complete, not lacking anything"* (James 1:2-4 NIV). We learned to pray and seek Him early in the morning. We learned that choosing God is choosing life. Our family and friends will benefit from our unselfishness. We ask God to increase (enlarge, add to) our faith (belief or trust in Him without logical proof). Here we are now being sifted (shaken, tempted, challenged) to see what's really in our heart. *"Simon, Simon, Satan has asked to sift you[ ] as wheat. But I have prayed for you, Simon, that your faith may not fail. And when you have turned back, strengthen your brothers"*(Luke 22:31-32 NIV).

Why didn't Jesus pray for Simon's pride, his attitude, or his mouth? Simon was known as a loud mouth, a prideful follower of Christ. So why did Jesus pray for Simon's faith? Satan is not as concerned about Simon's pride, his attitude or his mouth. Nor is Satan as concerned about whether you go to church or bible study. Nor is Satan as concerned about whether you smoke or drink alcohol. No, Satan is concerned about your faith! This is why Jesus prayed that Simon's faith does not fail. It is encouraging to know that Jesus is praying for us too, that our faith does not fail. However, He doesn't stop there. Jesus knows that there will be times when our faith is tested and we are shaken by it. Simon was more concerned about what people thought. This caused him to become fearful. Fear was in Simon's heart. So it is encouraging to know that we have an Intercessor in heaven that knows us and is praying for us! However, as we become to know (become familiar with) Jesus, we can trust Him in any situation. Knowing we are victorious in Christ Jesus, we can reach back and strengthen someone else, encourage someone else to trust Him. Let us help others become mature in their faith. For some of us, God raised us to do some things that seemed crazy or impossible. As we trust Him, our faith will increase. The key is to trust (believe, have complete confidence in) Him. *"By faith Noah, being divinely warned of things not yet seen, moved with godly fear, prepared an ark for the saving of his household, by which he condemned the world and became heir of the righteousness which is according to faith"*(Hebrews11:7 NIV).

*"Create in me a pure* (not mixed with any other substance; clean and free from impurities; complete) *heart, O God, and renew* (to make new spiritually; restore to freshness; rebuild) *a steadfast* (firmly fixed in place; immovable; not subject to change) *spirit* (blow; breathe; holy spirit) *within me"*(Psalm 51 NIV). Guess what? He will because our heart's desire is to know Him! Intimacy, Yes! See into me, see into my heart God!

**P**ray: Speak to God, listen to God and meditate on His Word

**R**elease: Let it out and let it go; get free by being honest

**E**ntrust: commit yourself to Him with confidence

**S**eek: Search for Him and find Him

**S**oak: Absorb Him and His Word; saturate yourself in Him and His Word.

Let Him remove your stains of guilt, (unforgiveness, anger, addiction, etc).

## About The Author

Elder Winnie Walker

*Elder Winnie Walker serves under the great leadership of Pastor Trena Stephenson of Woman of God Ministries (WofGod). She is also the Editor-in-Chief for the Daughters of Distinction Newsletter, a subsidiary of WofGod. Elder Winnie is very passionate about bringing people into an active and personal relationship with Jesus Christ through the Word of God, skits, plays, and life experiences. Her heart's desire is to empower and encourage all people through the Word of God to change from the inside out as they deal with life's challenges and to move people from spiritual infancy to Christ-like maturity. She is married to Derrell Walker (25 years), they have two adult children, and one grandchild.*

# Chapter 7

## *Be Still And Know*

*"Be still and know that I am God. I will be praised in all the nations; I will be praised throughout the earth."(Psalm 46:10 New Century Version NCV).*

What a title to be given to me by God himself "Be Still and Know". I wonder how many people have heard the Lord tell them "be still and know I'm God" and truly get the understanding of what God is saying. Well journey with me as we explore what God was telling me personally. First, let's start out by defining the words be, still and know:

**Be:** remain, stay, or exist;

**Still:** not moving, silently or without motion – adverb, peace or silence and;

**Know:** hold information in mind, be certain about something; realize something and comprehend something; have encountered somebody or something before.

Now I have a question for you: Have you ever been put into a position that you don't know totally what you are suppose to do but yet you're just standing and trusting God to lead, guide, and direct your path? God has the blueprint for your life because he is the master architect (a person who designs and guides a plan) that designed the blueprint in my life.

*"For I know the thoughts that I think toward you, says the LORD, thoughts of peace and not of evil, to give you a future and a hope."*(Jeremiah 29:11 NKJV).

A blueprint is like a map it shows you how to get to your designation by following the map. Sometimes you cause a delay which can keep you from getting to the next phase of completion. When a blueprint is designed by God, we should know what section of the blueprint needs to be completed first before going onto the next phase. We can look at this like building a house. You will see many different rooms that need to be built or completed before the next foundation is laid.

You must make sure the foundation is complete before building the house frame with wood. When God gives you a ministry, you must make sure the foundation is strong. *"Unless the LORD builds the house, They labor in vain who build it; Unless the LORD guards the city, The watchman stays awake in vain."*(Psalm 127:1 NKJV). He wants it built on the foundation of Christ, not yourself, your thoughts, motives, or anyone else. He wants to build according to the main details he gives you for the ministry. You must be prayerful and watchful for people that desire to attach themselves to the ministry. You must make sure their motives are in line with your vision and that they are not adding or taking away from the vision.

If you're not prayerful or watchful you will have vultures coming in to try to steal, kill, or destroy. You may not even realize their motive. God knows their intentions and he will put you in a position to "be still and know" while he works it out before the building gets destroyed, or vision gets wiped out.

Let me share with you what God told me one day. You are allowing too many people to speak into your ear that is causing a distraction to your vision and keeping you from hearing clearly from me. God told me to "be still" when I woke up the next morning because he was performing spiritual surgery on me. God had diagnosed my spiritual condition and told me what was hindering me. He told me that it had to be spiritually removed. God said He had to surgically remove some people that were attached to me in order to move to the next place spiritually place in Him. If you look at the act of surgery, it's performed in order to remove something that is affecting your physical health. Removing the problem will put you in a better physical state. This was a spiritual condition was that was affecting spiritually in my relationship with God. God conveyed that I had to be in agreement with what He is doing. He told me not to bring certain people back in my life. When people or situations are removed from you it puts you in position of staying focused and relying on God and to trust what He is doing with you.

I came to realize that God was pruning me, taking me through a pruning process.
*"I am the true vine, and My Father is the vinedresser. Every branch in Me that does not bear fruit He takes away; and every branch that bears fruit He prunes, that it may bear more fruit."*
(John 15:1-2 NKJV).
What is pruning? Merriam-Webster defines pruning as cutting off or cutting back parts of for better shape or more fruitful growth . God was cutting back some relationships and calling me to come higher in my relationship with Him. Sometimes we look at pruning as bad when it actually is a good thing. Pruning is God's way of making room in your life for more of more of what matters most in order for Him to get the glory. This pruning was for my own good. God was pruning me for the next level of bearing more fruit for the ministry. I had to see and hear from him the new people He was calling in place to grasp a hold of His vision for me to help continue

to build the vineyard to bear more fruit. He sent people for the next season of my journey for the building of the ministry for the next level. It's like the vinedresser working his vineyard growing grapes and as the branch produces grapes from the vine he cut it back in order for it to bear (produce) more fruit.

    I had to be still and know that God wasn't trying to show Himself strong on my behalf by delivering me out of a difficult situation. He was causing me to be still because of what was inside of me that needed to be removed. There were some things that needed to die spiritually inside me in order for me to continue to grow for the perfecting of his ministry. *"But let patience have its perfect work, that you may be perfect and complete, lacking nothing."* (James 1:4 NKJV). He led me to love at another level like never before and that is to love no matter how bad you are treated by them. It doesn't matter if they make you feel as though they are smarter than you because he called you to be a servant with no conditions or limitations. *"And whatever you do, do it heartily, as to the Lord and not to men, knowing that from the Lord you will receive the reward of the inheritance; for you serve the Lord Christ. But he who does wrong will be repaid for what he has done, and there is no partiality."* (Colossians 3:23-25 NKJV).

    What if God told you He wanted to bless you with a new car but he specifically told you not to purchase it until the month of June but you decided to purchase it in May instead. Come to find out if you would have waited until the month the Lord told you, you would have saved a thirteen hundred on your purchase. Now that you have purchase the car at a higher cost you have a higher car note than expected. If you had you waited and been patient you would be happier with your car note, instead of worrying about making the monthly payment. You stepped out because of emotions. You were excited about purchasing a new car but ignored God's timing of when to purchase it.

    He showed me He will fight your battles, if you allow Him. I was put in a very uncomfortable situation where many complaints were being brought against me and my staff. The complaints were coming so hard and very strong. I knew it was only an attack from the enemy to keep me off track and unfocused. I wanted so very badly to speak from my emotions. I had to "be still and know." He was letting patience have its perfect work within me. It seemed everyone else was able to give their opinions to management but my voice was silenced from being heard. As I was waiting on the Lord I asked him what I should do concerning this situation. I felt fearful as if I was going to lose my mind. I wanted to throw in the towel. It then I was reminded of II Timothy *"For God has not given us a spirit of fear, but of power and of love and of a sound mind."*(II Timothy 1:7 NKJV). I had to be reminded by the Holy Spirit, if God allowed me to encounter this situation that He would show himself mighty and bring me out. First my patience and trust had to be built in God in this area to see me through. God said in His word, *"I will never leave you nor forsake you."*(Hebrews 13:5 NKJV). I was waiting on the salvation of the Lord to deliver me from my enemies, yet at the same time, I wanted to defend myself. However, I continued to show love and kindness towards the individual who was making the complaints.

I woke up one morning to God guiding me to seek Psalm 26 for my spiritual well-being. He was letting me know daughter I hear your cry and plea within your spirit asking me to clear your name of the false accusations against you. The next morning, God told me to seek and receive Psalm 37. God was telling me to trust and wait patiently on Him to act on my behalf. He had it all under control but I had to trust the process. The pressure of the persecution didn't feel good but I stood on Psalms 26 and 37, until God moved on my behalf during this time of adversity. God let me know He heard my cries during this time. It was through him that I was able to stand strong even though I wanted to give the management position back because it was not worth all of the pressure and persecution. God had other plans. He was letting me know that He was still pruning me. The battle truly was His and at the right moment and time I would have an opportunity to speak and be heard, if I would not be weary in my well doing. *"And let us not grow weary while doing good, for in due season we shall reap if we do not lose heart."*(Galatians 6:9 NJKV). When the appointed time came the manager told me, "Don't worry about it, you work for me." That's what God is telling us his children/servants to stop worrying what others think or what they are saying about you because you belong to me.

No one can move you out of position if you are standing in God. If you move out of position on your own because of the pressure then you are stepping outside the will of God for your life and purpose. Don't be tricked by the enemy no matter how much the pressure and persecution comes. It comes with the territory of being a follower of Jesus Christ; he went through it too. Remember God will deliver you from the situation if you trust him to deliver you. Your stepping out of position at the non appointed time can affect others lives that are connected to you for God's purpose.

Look at my process. As a teenage girl I had a dream of seeing myself wearing suits and being a manager in an office environment. I didn't understand this dream because I never saw myself as being a manager. I just saw myself getting a job in order to survive. For one thing I didn't think I was smart enough. I had a speech problem and I was shy and afraid to speak. By the way, did I tell you I thought I wouldn't live to see my thirties. This dream was given to me by God. Why? He had a purpose for my life even when I didn't understand when he gave it to me.

I started my career out as a clerk-typist and worked my way through the ranks to become an IT Specialist, where I thought I had met my maximum financial potential. A coworker share with me a strange dream he had about me. He saw me getting a promotion and moving to another office. He was a little upset with me because I didn't tell him. We didn't have a close relationship with each other so I was confused by his comments. Shortly thereafter, there was a higher position became available in my area. God told me this position was for me and to apply for it immediately. I felt there were so many other people more qualified or next in line to receive a promotion. God told me this job is yours, therefore apply. I applied and received a promotion to Deputy IT Security Officer in 2005. When much is given, much is required. *"For everyone to whom much is given, from him much will be required."*(Luke 12:48).

As a servant and knowing the Lord's will much more is required of you than those who don't know the Lord. Knowing and obeying the will of God for your life sometime requires losing close friendships and family members may misunderstanding you. It can cause a separation from them. This separation is necessary so there is no interference with what the Lord is telling you. Knowing and obeying God's calling allowed me to continuously advance at work, including receiving a promotion to Branch Chief of the Customer Support Branch in 2010.

Accepting a chief position in my division was not about the money or the fact I will have a higher title. It was positioning and preparing me for my spiritual position as a Pastor called to shepherd the flock he has assigned to me. Taking this position was to help cultivate the calling to effectively manage, encourage, and empower people. Moving out of position would not only affect me but others attached to my assignment. I have noticed everything God has done in my life over the past 4 years has been parallel in the natural and spiritual as I was promoted on the job. I was also promoted spiritually shortly thereafter. It truly was about trusting God, being still and knowing God is God. He will and can do whatever he wants to do and how he wants to do it. There is nothing people can do or say to change the purpose.

God reminded me of the story of Joseph from the book Genesis. God had Joseph's divine blueprint for his life as well. Joseph went through a process of adversity before being (appointed) promoted. First he was put in a pit by his brothers (betrayal) and sold into slavery. Secondly, at Potiphar's House he was positioned as overseer of all servants at Potiphar's house and then framed as an adulterer by his wife. Thirdly, he was placed in prison and appointed as prison keeper over the prisoners and forgotten in prison. At the set and appointed time he was called forth out of prison to interpret Pharaoh's dream because of his gifting to interpret. Pharaoh, as well as the other leaders that appointed Joseph to a position, knew God was with him. Then Pharaoh appointed (promoted) Joseph as second in command over all Egypt. Joseph's adversity he went through help to develop him personally and to build trust with others. It helped to prove Joseph to trustworthy as a leader along with building his character, leadership skills and ability.

    Now as I close my chapter, I know where I am in my process of being appointed to the next position (I'm still waiting). Take note that the pruning, timing, standing in adversity and not to get stuck in the process is part of the blueprint for your life. Do you know where you are in this process?

## About The Author

Elder Tammy L. McNair

Elder Tammy L McNair is an anointed, gifted, and compassionate preacher and teacher of the Gospel of Jesus Christ. She is CEO and Founder of Sister Circle Ministries Inc. in Waldorf, MD under the leadership and spiritual covering of Pastor Trena Stephenson, Woman of God Ministries Inc. Sister Circle Ministries Inc. is a women ministry of Sisters in Christ learning and growing together in Christ. Sisters receive healing, restoration, deliverance, and embracing their spiritual gift(s) and calling to impact the Kingdom of God. Elder Tammy answered the call to ministry in October of 2001 and preached her initial sermon on October 10, 2003, "Meant to Live and Not Die". She was licensed to preach in June of 2004. Elder Tammy has a heart to serve God's people with humility, pureness, integrity and to encourage them in the Lord. Elder Tammy has served in different areas of ministry. She has served as an intercessor and lead servant of a Prayer Ministry, Net ministry, and Marriage Ministry. She has preached at prayer breakfasts and has served on panels at women's conference. She is married to a Man of God Keith R McNair Sr. of 18 years and through their union have three beautiful gifts from God, Vanessa Keira (20), Keith Robert. Jr. (17), and Joseph Isaiah (10).

Email: www.SisterCircle2003@aol.com
Web Site: www.SCMinistries04.com
Ministry Line: 240-346-0056

# Chapter 8

*Stop Trippin!*

    First let us define the word "trippin." Urban Dictionary defines it as: overreacting or getting bent out of shape over something small; to become upset over small insignificant matters; or to allow an incident that can be solved peacefully to become blown out of context.

    Don't get bent out of shape when things don't go your way. Before approaching this subject I had to go to God in prayer, because this was a word for me. I had to do some deep soul searching within myself to bring this out. You see I am the one that will jump the boat before it takes off. I will take a matter to a whole another level; then I have to go back and apologize because of my actions. Don't Trip! There may be people on your job that are put in your life to break those things that God wants to strip from you, so that you may become more like him. You must be aware because the enemy walks about like a roaring lion seeking to devour whom he may! *"Be sober; be vigilant; because your adversary the devil walks about like a roaring lion, seeking whom he may devour."*(I Peter 5:8 NKJV). If you recognize that he is trying to sink you, then you have the gift of prayer to pray for strength to overcome his tactics.  He has many of them.  God wants to make you shine like pure gold.  You can't shine cursing and fussing out everybody on the job, or at home.  You know that you can tell someone off and not say a curse word and it is the same as cursing.  I want to tell you where God brought me from, he brought me from the foulest mouth ever to walk the earth, and he changed my language.  As Pastor Stephenson says, when we got saved we just changed partners but some of that old sin nature is still in us and it must be burned off, then God can use us like he really wants to use us.

    I know he still hears because he heard the cries and prayers of my mother and my girlfriend.  They prayed me out of the pits of hell.  I got saved and baptized in the year of 2001, and I have not stopped running for my life yet.  He blessed me with a husband in 2004, and together we are running for Jesus.  I want you know that Rome was not built in a day, God is still working on me and through me.  He is doing it today; you may be a leader in ministry, and you may have regressed back to that old sin nature , meaning we may have said something mean, or told someone off, and hurt someone's feelings, Stop trippin!  Go to God in Prayer and ask his forgiveness, make a point of controlling you temper.  Merriam-Webster Dictionary defines self control  as the checking of one's true feelings and impulses when dealing with others.  You must go back and apologize to that person and make a point of not returning to the same behavior, it easier said than done.  When you encounter an explosive situation remove yourself from the situation or exercise restraint.  Do not respond to what may have been said or totally ignore the situation.  If someone constantly wrongs you and takes advantage of you, don't leave a nasty email or voice mail, trust me it will come back to bite you.

    I experienced the most humbling learning experience when  I left a nasty voice mail to some people that I interact with in ministry.  Once this voice mail was replayed in the presence of my Pastor I felt like a little cartoon character reduced to a pebble.  I felt so small and stupid that I immediately repented and apologized for my actions. I decided that if I get upset or angry about a situation or feel that things are going not as planned before I go to the drama queen level, I will go to God in prayer. Even though I may be hurting, or feel that I have been wronged I go to God in Prayer. I ask for his strength to deal with whatever is bothering me. The scripture says: *"Be angry and do not sin , do not let the sun go down on your wrath, nor give place to the devil."*(Ephesians 4:26-27 NKJV). When you start trippin people around you will start to avoid you. They will label you the "drama queen" you don't want to wear a label for the rest of your life. The Urban Dictionary defines the word "drama queen" as: someone who turns something unimportant into a major deal or blows things way out of proportion whenever the chance is given.

    You know this is a word for me in this season of my life. There is an area on my job that I really don't like working, I would really get bent out of shape when asked to cover the area, but the Holy Spirit is saying to me stop trippin. It is an assignment that God has given you. There is someone that God wants you to help; there is a path that must be crossed. This is part of your assignment. Someone is there waiting for your encouragement. We are being watched and we must be an example not only in words but in deeds. We may be asked to do what we think is a menial job, however all jobs are important in the kingdom. Stop trippin! The first time you act out of order the people on your job or in your church will remember that you lost your temper. They will quickly forget anything nice, pleasant, or encouraging you may have done. Remember first impressions are lasting ones. Don't let the last thing you are remembered for getting heated if someone asks you to do something not listed in your job description. Keep a smile at all times and be ready to assist whenever and wherever necessary. It is not what you do. It is how you do it and your reaction when asked to do it.

    Take a look at the book of Proverbs it reads: *"Pride [goeth] before destruction and a haughty spirit before a fall.*(Proverbs 16:18

KJV), in other words having a haughty spirit can cause us to trip or fall. We should be humble and lowly in spirit. Having put on the garment of meekness, y'all know I am preaching to myself. I am no better than anyone, I have to repent daily. The first part of this scripture says pride goeth before destruction. I am appealing to you today; don't be destroyed because of your attitude. Remember people are human and make mistakes. You are not so important that you don't make mistakes. Don't be so hard on someone because they made a mistake. Don't act out of character because you may feel you have been looked over. I know a lot about this subject because I can act ugly when I think I have been wronged. I am trying to help someone, please look at this scenario: I recently placed an order at my pharmacy and the staff could not get my order correct. I became frustrated with the pharmacy and started to vent my frustration to the staff. I went home calmed down and asked God to forgive me for my actions. The next I called pharmacy and calmly explained the situation. Once they understood my request, the staff apologized and filled my order. A few days later I sent a card to the two young ladies at the pharmacy to thank them for helping me even though I was being a difficult customer. Put on the garment of meekness, robe yourselves with humbleness of heart and you will reap a huge reward. Don't get yourself worked up over nothing or raise your blood pressure to the boiling point. You are just hurting yourself.

*"Let this mind be in you which was also in Christ Jesus."*
(Philippians 2:5 NKJV).

You think about potentially explosive situations, you should calm down and think of ways to make it smooth or calm. Here is an example of how this may be done: It may be that you have to walk away until an hour or another day has passed. Go to the individual or individuals in question and talk over what took place and how it could be done better. Remember if the situation becomes explosive, you may react to it and start trippin. That is not a good reaction. Sometimes situations and things are premeditated

to see if you will start trippin! Don't become Satan's victim reacting to things that he is looking for you to react to, be watchful!
*"Resist him, steadfast in the faith, knowing that the same sufferings are experienced by your brotherhood in the world."*
(I Peter 5:9 NKJV).
Don't react, pray a short prayer and walk out with a smile even though it may be like someone is belting you in your gut. Walk with your head up, keep smiling and confuse the enemy! Always keep these words upon your lips in dealing with situations that may arise against you, "Lord in the name of Jesus, Let no weapon against me prosper, nor my family, nor my job, nor my household in the Name of Jesus, AMEN!"

Even in ministry you will be tested. Sometimes you may get out of line with your leader or those who have the lead over you. You may think you have been overlooked in promotion, and are about to leave, stop trippin, stay put, get on your knees, and develop your prayer life. If we look in the Bible at the story of David at I Samuel chapter 16:11-13, David was anointed to be the next king of Israel. Upon receiving his anointing David did not trip, but remained humble. He continued to trust God; he continued to do what God instructed him to do. When we look at I Samuel 16: 21-23 David became Saul's Armor bearer. An example of this would be if God spoke to you and told you he was elevating you to Pastor, however the Bishop appoints you as Assistant Pastor. You know that God spoke to you and said you are a Pastor, but you need training. You may think you have arrived, don't trip, take the appointment, and keep your notepad handy. Take notes and do lots of observing, because you never know when you are called to step in on behalf of the Pastor or circumstances may change. Just remain humble. You must respect the anointing that God has placed over your leader's life. You must respect those who have the lead over your souls. In all situations remain humble, avoid the spirit of haughtiness. Sometimes we find ourselves in situations that we are being taken advantage of, whatever advice they are giving it should always be bible based, at no time should it be of their own opinion. Leaders should at all times refer to the bible for guidance and direction, in this way you will not be leading the sheep astray. You must exercise wisdom and the spirit of meekness. Clothe yourself with it, you will get better results. You will help someone in the meantime get blessed as well. I was in a situation where I left before my time. I was out there a lost sheep. I latched onto the wrong thing, but God dealt with me on the threshing floor, He chastised me and gave me specific instructions. Merriam-Webster defines the word "thresh " as to separate seed from a harvested plant mechanically also: to separate seed in this way. If we look at this from an agricultural standpoint, threshers are used for separating seed from the plan. More modern combine cuts, threshes and cleans the grain. The floor is where you lay prostrate faced down, and listen for God's voice. In this context the "threshing floor" represents when God who is the thresher, acts as the threshing machine separating those wheat and weeds in our life, he strips off what he does not need and adds what he wants to make us more like him. He separates us and put us apart for his service. I obeyed his instructions and now I am free. I stayed in prayer and learned a valuable lesson; keep God as the director of your paths and you won't trip. He won't lead you astray.

    God has spoke to me and said some of you are trippin because you don't know how to get free. You don't know when you are out line. Some of you have been doing it for years and don't know you are going down the wrong path. There is enough work in the kingdom of God for everyone to do something. This may be the season for you to set down and really develop your prayer life. If you are called to minister don't get a church thinking you are going to get offerings. Stop trippin, you need to assist the Pastor and learn how to shepherd God's people. Don't trip because you are not the one called to pray the main prayer of the service, read the scripture or the Pastor did not pick you to be on the program. Thank God. Let someone else have a chance to work in the ministry. Others in the church need instruction and exposure as well. You are not the only one God is using at this time. *"And other sheep I have, which are not of this fold: them also I must bring, and they shall hear my voice; and there shall be one fold, and one shepherd."*(John 10:16 KJV). Be interceding they may need your prayers. Don't take on the spirit of jealousy it will hinder your ministry.

To sum it all up, we start trippin for various reasons: families, work, home, friends, so called friends, and relationships with anyone me may come in contact with in our daily lives. We must maintain our integrity. First to God, we represent Him. He is the one who saved us from a life of destruction. God saved our souls from heartache and despair. When you find yourself in situations such as I have described or worse, the first thing to do is fall on your knees, and ask forgiveness, repent, turnaround from your way of thinking and change for the better. Trust me no one will want to be around if you act like a "drama queen". I am praying each day that I show and display the spirit of Christ Jesus our Lord. Trust me when you have acted out of character and others know you are a Christian, some will not let you live it down. If you rectify it with the Father who is in Heaven and confess your sins openly, He is the one who will forgive. Ask God to continue to walk and talk to you daily. As the lyrics of the hymn, Garden of Prayer state: "I come to the garden alone, while the dew is still on the roses, and the voice I hear falling on my ear, the son of God discloses, Yes He walks with me and He talks with me and He tells me I am His own and the joy we share as we tarry there, none other has ever known." Spend quality time with the Father in the Garden of Prayer, wherever your garden may be, in your home, in the bathroom of your job, in a peaceful place in the park or by the waters. Go to God in prayer and He alone will be your guide.

# About The Author

### Evangelist Yvonne Maria Nock

*Evangelist Yvonne Maria Nock is an ordained Evangelist under the awesome leadership of Pastor Trena Stephenson, Woman of God Ministries, Inc. Evangelist Nock was saved and filled with the Holy Spirit in the year of 2001. She answered the call of ministry in the year of 2007, as a traveling evangelist; she is a workshop facilitator, preacher, teacher, praise and worship leader. Worship is her passion. In the year of May of 2008 she appeared with her Pastor as co-host of "Daughter's of Distinction Live Broadcast, doing the Medical Moment, from that spot "Being Fit 4 Life in the Kingdom Broadcast was birthed. She is the host and executive producer of that show. This show is to educate men and women, pastors and leaders in the kingdom of God about their bodies and how to take care of our temples. Her interests include, entertaining and cooking. She loves to do liturgical and prophetic dance. Evangelist Nock is the daughter of Juanita Wilson-Winston and the late Donald Green, she is married to the love of her life, Deacon Anthony Nock and has one son, Derek M. Davis. She loves taking care of people and helping people get the health care they deserve.*

*My desire is grow older in God, to become more mature, less of me and more of HIM. One of my favorite scripture is: Psalm 61:2 – "From the end of the earth will I cry unto thee, when my heart is overwhelmed: lead me to the rock [that] is higher than I."*

# Chapter 9

## Holiness Is Required

The word holy means set apart, distinct, or different. The holiness of God reaches far beyond any man's comprehension. He is God all by Himself. He is unique and above all of His creation. Holiness is a life style and we must practice holiness day by day because there is no way that we can have a close walk with God without first being holy. *"Mortify (put to death) therefore your members which are upon the earth; fornication, uncleanness, inordinate affection, evil concupiscence, and covetousness, which is idolatry."* (Colossians 3:5 KJV).

Holiness must be in the inner most part of our being. God is holy and cannot tolerate sin. He is not accepting any excuses for sin. Therefore we must hate sin as God hates sin. Holiness is required and as the people of God, we must be distinctively different. The light of God in us must shine through us so that the world can see the Christ in us.

In order to achieve spiritual growth we need to *"Study to show thyself approved unto God, a workman that needeth not be ashamed, rightly dividing the Word of God."* (II Timothy 2:15 KJV).

Meditate on the scriptures fast and pray. Take time to sit in His presence being quiet and listening for His voice. Make love to God. Praise His wonderment and magnificence.

God is longing to use us in supernatural ways like never before. It is time to rise and shine. God desires to perfect everything that concerns us. We must be holy to meet the approval of God and to receive what God has destined for our lives. Every test, trial and tribulation we encounter is just another stepping stone to catapult us to where God would have us to go in Him.

How do we become holy? We become holy by conforming to the image of Christ and becoming like him. We must separate ourselves from all evil. The sin in our lives must be conquered and annihilated. God requires holiness and holiness requires purity. *"For the grace of God that bringeth salvation hath appeared to all men, teaching us that, denying ungodliness and worldly lust, we should live soberly, righteously, and godly, in this present time, looking for that blessed hope, and the glorious appearing of the great God and Savior Jesus Christ. Who gave himself for us, that he might redeem us from all iniquity, and purify unto himself a peculiar people, zealous of good works."*(Titus 2:11-14 KJV).
God desires for us to come into maturity and be no more children tossed to and fro, and carried about with every wind of doctrine. The Holy Bible is God's written Word. It is what we need to study and meditate on. Knowing the Word of God will alleviate false doctrines and practices.

If we are walking with God, we should not be satisfied with anything less than 100% of what God has for us. We should reach in the spirit and grab our blessings because God is restoring to us what the enemy has taken. We are getting it all back and some more. I believe this is the season for new ministries to be birthed and an abundance of favor to be poured out on the people of God. God is a relational God. He wants his people to spend time with him in prayer. It is good to set aside a special place and time to meet God each day. Start your prayer off praising God for being good, wonderful and majestic. Let him know how much you love him and appreciate and adore him.

Our relationship with God should be so personal and intimate that God will speak to us on a daily basis. He is always communicating with us, but are we tuned into his frequency? If we would only take time to be still in his presence and relieve our minds from the hustle and bustle of the day. We would be able to hear God and hear him clearly.

The first level of how God speaks to us is through the word of God, the Holy Bible. All scripture is given by inspiration of God, and is profitable for doctrine, reproof, correction, and instruction in righteousness.

Let's first look at revelation. There is an example of God speaking revelation in Joel. *"And it shall come to pass after, that I pour out of my spirit upon all flesh; and your sons and daughters shall prophesy, your old men shall dream dreams, your young men shall see visions."*(Joel 2:28 KJV). Joel could not have known this without God revealing it to him. Just as Joel received revelation from God, we should also receive revelation from God.

God also speaks to his people through dreams as in Numbers. *"And he said, Hear now my words, If there be a prophet among you, I the Lord will make myself known unto him in a vision, and will speak unto him in a dream."*(Numbers 12:6 KJV). In order to hear God, we have to quiet our spirit. Once our spirit is quiet we can hear God speak. The dreams that we dream coming from God is a source of revelation another way in which God speaks to us.

Another way that God speaks is through prophecy as in Jeremiah *"Then the Lord put forth his hand, and touched my mouth, and the Lord said unto me, Behold, I have put my words in thy mouth."*(Jeremiah 1:9 KJV). God downloads a revelation to a prophetic person to speak forth what He has given him or her to speak into the life of a person/nation. etc. We must speak only what God has told us to speak. We are never to add anything to what

God has given us.

God speaks to us in impressions using our five senses of sight, hearing, taste, smell and touch. Impressions are perceived. An example is found in the Book of Mark. *"And immediately when Jesus perceived in his spirit that they so reasoned within themselves, he said unto them, why reason ye these things in your heart?"*(Mark 2:8 KJV). There are times that we perceive something through our senses and think that it is our imagination. God uses our senses to convey a message to us. Pay attention to your senses so that you don't miss the revelation. Some people will hear God by an audible voice as in Isaiah. *"And thine ears shall hear a word behind thee, saying, This is the way, walk ye in it, when ye turn to the right hand, and when ye turn to the left."*(Isaiah 30:21 KJV). God speaks in the ear of some people.

Have you ever had an angelic visitation? Angles do visit people and the proof is in the book of Hebrews. *"Be not forgetful to entertain strangers: for thereby some have entertained angels unawares."*(Hebrews 13:2 KJV). You may have heard stories about people being translated in the spirit. I like to refer to it as an out of the body experience. We can read of such an experience in Corinthians. *"I knew a man in Christ above fourteen years ago, whether in the body, I cannot tell; or whether out the body, I cannot tell; God knoweth such an one caught up to the third heaven, the abode of God."*(II Corinthians 12:2-4 KJV).

God will speak through visions. Visions happen when we are awake. We can read of such a vision in Acts. *"On the morrow, as they went on their journey, and drew nigh unto the city, Peter went up upon the housetop to pray about the sixth hour: And he became very hungry, and would have eaten: but while they made ready he fell into a trance and saw heaven opened, and a certain vessel descending unto him, as it had been a great sheet knit at the four corners, and let down to the earth: Wherein were all manner of four-footed and wild beast, and creeping things, and fowls of the air. And there came a voice to him, rise Peter, kill and eat. But*

*Peter said, not so Lord; for I have never eaten anything that is common or unclean. And the voice spake unto him again the second time, what God hath cleansed, that call not thou common. This was done twice: and the vessel was received up again into heaven. Now while Peter doubted in himself what this vision which he had seen should mean, the men were sent from Cornelius had made enquiry for Simons house, and stood before the gate, and called, and asked whether Simon, which was surnamed Peter, were lodged there."* (Acts 10:9-18 KJV). When God gives you a vision it's like watching television only you are seeing with your spiritual eyes. I have not touched on all the ways that God speaks, however I pray that what I did speak on will enlighten and encourage you in our journey.

When I started some years ago as a hospital chaplain there were some things that I experienced that I did not understand. I did not know that God was giving me a word of knowledge. I visited a patient who had asked for prayer. Standing next to her bed I held her hand and began to pray for her. I cut the prayer short because I began to feel sick and a lot of pain came on my body. What I didn't know at the time is that God was giving me a word of knowledge as to what I needed to pray for. The pain and sickness that I was feeling in my body was not my pain and sickness, but what the patient was experiencing in her body. It was a word of knowledge to me.

Another experience was an extreme feeling of nervousness upon entering the room of a patient without touching him. I prayed for the patient but did not realize that once again God was giving me a word of knowledge. Our spirit must be sensitive to the Spirit of God so that He is able to communicate with us. God speaks, we must learn to listen.

The Church (body of Christ) must come to maturity. The five fold gifts or ascension gifts are apostle, prophet, evangelist, pastor and teacher. The purpose of the gifts is to build up the saints and equip the body of Christ for the work of the ministry. (Ephesians 4:11 KJV). It is time to get serious and make a commitment to be holy.  Holiness my brothers and sisters carries with it a standard.  We can't just live any kind of way.  If we are going be holy as God is holy, we must do as God says.  Surely we will have to make some sacrifices and life style changes, but every sacrifice and change will be to our benefit.

How can we be holy?  I believe Peter gives us the answer. *"The Lord is not slack concerning His promise, as some count slackness, but is longsuffering toward us, not willing that any should perish but that all should come to repentance.  But the day of the Lord will come as a thief in the night, in which the heavens will pass away with a great noise, and the elements will melt with fervent heat; both the earth and the works that are in it will be burned up. Therefore, since all these things will be dissolved, what manner of persons ought you to be in holy conduct and godliness, looking for and hastening the coming of the day of God, because of which the heavens will be dissolved, being on fire, and the elements will melt with fervent heat."*(II Peter 3:9-12 KJV).

Take a look at what the book of Hebrews has to say: *"Further more we have had fathers of our flesh which corrected us, and we gave them reverence: shall we not much rather be in subjection unto the Father of spirits, and live.  For they verily for a few days chastened us after their own pleasure; but he for our profit that we might be partakers of his holiness.  Now No chastening for the present seemeth to be joyous, but grievous: nevertheless afterward it yieldeth the peaceable fruit of righteousness unto them which are exercised thereby.  Wherefore Lift up the hands which hang down, and the feeble knees; and make straight paths for your feet, lest that which is lame be turned out of the way; but let it rather be healed.  Follow peace with all men, and holiness, without which no man shall see the Lord."*(Hebrews 12:9-14 KJV).

Holiness is required, be ye holy, and let God use you as he pleases.  Fulfill the destiny, purpose and potential that God has placed in you before you were in your mother's womb.  Let God get a return on the deposit he has deposited in you. Remember! Holiness is required.

## About The Author

### Pastor Sandra Hill

*Sandra Hill is the senior pastor and founder of "Power and Destiny Ministries, Inc" located in Baltimore, Maryland, a ministry of reconciliation where everybody is somebody. She is spiritually covered and accountable to Apostle James D. Nelson presiding prelate and founder of World Assemblies of Restoration. Pastor Hill was under the pastorate of Apostle Nelson for over 20 years before launching out to pastor. She is a staff chaplain in a well known medical center as well as a female prison. Her passion is to win as many souls as she can for the Kingdom of God. She is about kingdom building.*

# Chapter 10

*Operating Under An
Open Heaven*

There is a realm of God's glory and power that transforms and empowers our lives and makes us effective instruments in God' hand when operating under an open heaven. An open heaven is an opportunity created by our heavenly Father, where the Holy Spirit makes evident the work of the cross. , The physical evidence of an open heaven is seen and the favor of the Lord is revealed in the Book of Ezekiel, chapter 1. God's people will no longer just believe a doctrine, but will have encounters with God for themselves. God is sending forth His sons and daughters empowered from heaven to establish His kingdom on earth as it is in heaven. The Holy Spirit who dwells in you will lead, guide and direct your every step. You will purpose to live according to His desires; for it's no longer you that lives, but Christ living through you. Your mind will be set on and seeking the things that will edify the body of Christ. You must have a teachable spirit, able to walk by faith and not by sight, and most importantly, you must walk in the love of Christ towards others. My question to you is twofold – Are you operating under an open heaven, if not, Are you willing to make the necessary changes in your life to walk in the authority and blessings that are yours under an open heaven? You will have free access to everything in the heavenly realm, a free flowing of God's abundant grace and power.

The power of God begun to function in the ministry of Jesus after heaven opened (Matthew 3:16-17 NKJV). God's manifested glory will be revealed in and through you in all of its majesty as it is in heaven. Our prayer should be, "Lord, transform me into your image that I may reflect your glory. Reveal to me and through me that which will effect and bring change to our world." In this hour of transition, living and operating under an open heaven, the outer man (flesh) must die in order for our inner man (spirit) to live. Christ is calling for death to our thoughts, attitudes and actions as we become the full expression of His love. God is not asking us to live our lives for Him, but He is asking us to decease that He may live His life through us. In this dispensation, the Holy Spirit has been commissioned to activate and propagate the prophetic revelation gifts within the body of Christ to fulfill the pattern of His plan and purpose for this generation *"Oh that you would rend the heavens. That you would come down! That the mountains may shake at Your Presence"* (Isaiah 64:1-2 NKJV). During the past twenty-five years, God has revealed to me some of His plans for my life and for His church through prophetic revelation in spiritual writings. Come with me and allow me to share some of the things God has revealed to me. My heart's desire is that God will open your spiritual ears and eyes; as you receive His wisdom.

In this 21st century with all of its modern technology, one cannot function without the proper tools. There is the computer, digital television, iPod, GPS, cell phone, etc. Even with all these means of communication, they sometimes malfunction; computers crash, digital televisions lose power, and cell phones lose their signals if towers are not strong enough or out of range. Did you know that there are also tools necessary to operate under an open heaven? These tools which are mandatory include; discipline, obedience, humility, faith and love. Unlike our earthly tools, these are guaranteed to work forever, and have unlimited resources. These tools open the windows and doors of heaven. Heaven is never out of range to receive earth's signals. Earth air waves always tune into the right frequency for intimate relationship and communication with the heavenly Father. God has an open door policy, 24 hours a day, 7 days a week, 365 days a year. There are no missed calls, no static; the channel is always fine tuned, listening for your voice. You call, God hears! God calls, you hear! Are you listening for His voice? Have you called Him lately? When heaven calls, earth listens and obeys. When earth calls heaven, signs and wonders occur and blessing are poured out upon the earth. During a signs and wonders conference in Toronto, Canada, my heavenly Father shared these words with me, "this is a city of life, and this church lives under an open heaven." When you operate under an open heaven, there are always signs and wonders, healing, deliverance and a harvest of souls. God will reveal to you, as He has to me, the mysteries of His kingdom. The mysteries and treasures of heaven will begin to open and unfold before your spiritual eyes. You must have hearts that are open to receive, and minds that will believe as God pours out upon His church in this season.

There is an open heaven above you today. The heavenly Father is calling us individually and corporately to a higher level in Him. He is calling the natural realm to enter the supernatural realm. He is calling you up to a higher realm in His Spirit where He will reveal Himself to you. As you spend time in His presence, your spiritual eyes will be opened and your spiritual ears will be in tune to His voice. Your faith and spirit will manifest in the natural what you are seeing and experiencing in the supernatural. A new power and energy will be available to you. We have to believe beyond our own natural understanding and limitations, and see things as God sees them. God is doing a new thing, and He is doing it in a new way. The time is coming – it has in fact come – when what you are will not matter, and where you go to worship will not matter. It's who you are and the way you live that counts before God. *"Your worship must engage your spirit in the pursuit of truth. That's the kind of people the Father is out looking for; those who are simply and honestly themselves before Him in their worship. God is sheer being itself-Spirit, and those who worship Him must do it out of their very being, their spirit, their true selves in adoration."*(John 4:23-24, Message).

God wants to move in the body of Christ in a supernatural way. In the Bible, God spoke to His people, and not just the prophets, in different ways. One of the most common manifestations of operating under an open heaven is receiving prophetic revelation and experiences. God will take the fear out of the idea of the spirit realm and spirit visitations if you ask Him. He will help you to see how natural it is to communicate in the heavenly realm. *"It shall come to pass afterward that I will pour out My Spirit on all flesh; your sons and your daughters shall prophesy, your old men shall dream dreams, your young men shall see visions. And also on my menservants and on my maidservants, I will pour out My Spirit in those days."*(Joel 2: 28-29 NKJV).
There is a supernatural shifting in the atmosphere in this season. God is changing attitudes and developing His attributes in the lives of His people to receive His blessings. Are you ready to receive all the blessings God has for your life? Jesus said,

*"The truth is you will all see heaven open and the angels of God going up and down upon the Son of man."*(John 1:51, NKJV).
Jesus is our ladder between heaven and earth, and without Him there is no open heaven. Under an open heaven you will begin to see manifestations of God's divine intervention in your family, church, community, city and country. God activated into reality His eternal purpose when He made earth and created man in His image. When God created you, He patterned you after Himself. He wants to use you in His plan and purpose for your life. Are you in alignment to receive your new assignment? Are you waiting for an

angelic visitation to give you divine instructions? This is a kairos moment (the opportune or right time) don't miss it! God is calling his church to seek His face daily. "Call to me and I will answer you, and show you great and mighty things, fenced and hidden which you do not know (do not distinguish and recognize, have knowledge of or understand) (Jeremiah 33:3, Amplified Version AMP). We need to develop an ear to hear what the spirit is saying to the church.

God is rending the heavens and making Himself known. To receive the deeper things of God, you must sit at His feet and listen with spiritual ears. There must be a time of quietness and silence so you can hear what the Spirit is saying to receive a deeper revelation of His word. We are now stepping over into the glory of His manifested presence. The power of God is arising within you as you are transformed from glory to glory. The Kingdom of heaven is invading earth, and it is coming through the Holy Spirit. When your spirit comes into alignment with the Holy Spirit it is a Spirit to spirit connection. It is a divine connection, where time and destiny meets. If you are in the right place, at the right time, His blessings will overtake you. Are you prepared to receive the manifestation of an open heaven today? The word of God tells us to be diligent in keeping our hearts pure and clean, for out of the heart spring the issues of life. The spirit of man is the lamp of the Lord, searching all the inner depths of the heart.

As children of God, you have an inheritance that is yours to receive right now. There is a purpose that He has predestined just for you. This provision was made through an inheritance that He has given and prepared for you through the death and resurrection of His Son, Jesus Christ. This inheritance is both natural and supernatural. The Holy Spirit is here to give you God's inheritance that was predestined for your life to complete the work He prepared beforehand. There is a supernatural provision hidden deep in the things of God that can only be uncovered and unlocked by the Holy Spirit. It is time to activate the supernatural in your life if you plan to operate under an open heaven. I encourage you today to draw closer to God, and allow the Holy Spirit to become your teacher. He will not only activate the supernatural in your life, but will also bring forth those things that He has revealed to you by faith, in the Spirit. Begin to expect the unexpected. He meets all of your needs, and gives you all your needs to do what He has called you to do. This is a wonderful and exciting time for the body of Christ to live in. Since you were birthed out of the Sprit of God, you are to be lead and directed by the Holy Spirit, creating what we desire on earth by the Spirit in the realm of the Spirit. Heaven and earth move in response to the spoken word of God. He has placed ministering angels to answer to the words of faith that are released from your mouth. When we pray out of our spirit, live in the Spirit, and speak His living word, Jesus will move heaven and earth to align itself with His spoken word. Did you know that prayer protects and shapes your heart (total being) in the right direction towards God? It is time to renew your mind, and receive the mind of Christ in you. You will have to fall in love with Jesus all over again, as you did when He first came into your life. Few of you have realized that your heavenly Father's heart longs for companionship of His children. Every spiritual encounter is about intimacy with Jesus. Spending time in His presence praying and fasting is one of the most powerful tools to operating under an open heaven.

  Did you know that as you get into position and resume the correct posture God will grant you divine favor? *"O come, let us worship and bow down. Let us knell before the Lord our maker. For He is our God."*(Psalm 95: 6, NKJV). Be still and know that He is God. When you stay focus on Him you will began to walk with clarity of vision. In the book of Genesis chapter 28, Jacob had a dream in which he saw a ladder, a stairway that was set up on the earth. It reached an open heaven where he saw the angels of God ascending and descending on it, and God stood above it. You may ask the question, why did he have that dream? What did it mean? Sometimes God has to put us in a quiet place to talk to us, because we become so busy with worldly things. Therefore, He has to talk to us through dreams and visions. He had a message to give to Jacob which would affect the rest of his life. He had a plan, a purpose, and a pattern to fulfill through Jacob that would change lives. His promises to Jacob were: *"I am the Lord, the God of Abraham your grandfather and the God of Isaac. I will give you and your descendants the land on which you are now sleeping. Your descendants will be as the dust of the earth. They will spread west and east, north and south, and all the families of the earth will be blessed through you and your descendants. I am with you and will protect you everywhere you go, and will bring you back to this land. I will not leave you until I have done what I promised you."* (Genesis 28:13-15 NCV). His convenient promise is not only for Jacob, but it is also for us, as we develop a personal and intimate relationship with Him. You too can receive your covenant promises as you come into alignment with His plan, His purpose and His pattern for your life. "Saturate your soul in the oil of My Spirit, for through My people shall the eternal glory of the Father be manifested unto the nations. For the everlasting power of the Godhead is incarnate in My chosen ones. Is it not written that the kingdom of God dwelleth within you? In the day that you make Me Lord in thy life and give to Me the scepter and allow Me to reign within; then I will begin to move, and My power shall radiate forth from thine entire being. Then will I bring to pass miracles." When we humble ourselves and repent, God will work miracles as we operate under His open heaven.

## About The Author

Apostle June A, Hunter
Affectionately known as "Mother June"

*Mother June is an ordained apostle and minister of the gospel, who was prophetically provoked to come forth through divine revelation. God spoke to her through prophetic men of God regarding her ministry with hurting women in leadership. He led her from CBN University (currently Regent University) in Virginia Beach, Virginia, where she counseled students in Christian affairs, and led intercessory prayer groups with faculty and students—He told her to "Go Feed My Sheep" in Petersburg, Virginia. God has given this Jewel in His Crown, the gift of the five fold ministry for the perfecting, equipping and building up of the body of Christ. She is the founder and administrator of ATOM (Agape Teas Outreach Ministries). Teach My Word, Exalt My Name, Affirm My Love, and Service My People (TEAS). From ATOM, God birthed prophetic teas, intercessory prayer group, mountain retreats, seminars, community outreach, and Bible study. Mother June also has a boot camp for prophetic ministers and prophets. She is highly sought after for her spiritual wisdom and revelation from all of her children, both here and abroad.*

*Mother June is overseer and spiritual advisor for many ministries. She mentors God's sheep, activating their spiritual gifts through prophetic revelation. She teaches them to love and trust God, building their faith. Her greatest fulfillment is to push you through the birth canal of life, compelling you to come forth in your ministry.*
 Apostle June A. Hunter – atomjh@aol.com – 804-732-3123

# Chapter 11

## Unstopping The Blockages

*Shattering glass windows.*
*Shattering glass ceilings.*
*To be able to fully partake of the fresh winds of God.*
*Removing the barriers of the heart that take captive our souls and restrict our spirits.*
*Pushing through the pain and reaching upwards.*
*Upwards, towards a God who is waiting with a passion for us to realize the potential within.*
*To realize that our realities are not God's rationalization of what it is to live freely,*
*Walking in the liberty of the Creator's love.*

Walking in liberty begins with overcoming our past. We do this by being courageous enough to see ourselves as wounded individuals. Being wounded, we have adopted various coping techniques in order to accommodate our pain. God still hears but are we really opening up a line of open, honest dialogue? When we speak are we conveying our deepest fears? Do we convey the depth of heartache and sorrow that have brought us to places of hidden stagnancy in various parts of our lives? These hidden places become blockages that hold us hostage to self-indifference. We become content and complacent because it is easier to busy ourselves with the task of today; then to get quiet with God, look deep within, and give him a transparent view of ourselves. It is not for the Creator that this must be done, but for us. Only with a keen awareness of self can God truly use us without the blemishes of life scarring the ministries and love that pour from us. If we do not become real with God we are leaking vessels; never truly walking in the fullness of what has been ordained for our lives. Not seeing ourselves prevents us from walking in spirit and in truth. God is still listening; but have we come to places of pious privacy that prevent us from speaking what is real and true?

There is a keen awareness in the body of Christ that something must change, but what? We lack the capacity to keep persons engaged, active and alert to the spirit and passions of God. We change our services, add new programs and reach out to communities near and far. Still persons within our congregations go hurting and yearning for more. Some of us climb the ladder of what appears to be spiritual success to become tired, burned out, bitter, and angry. What we supposed would be the ultimate high has become a burden to maintain. We smile, putting on a happy face while slowly fading away from the inside out. Then there are those of us who just leave because we don't care to live the required facade. We seek that place in God where we experience peace, even in the midst of chaos. *"It is a place of peace that surpasses even our own understanding."*(Philippians 4:7 New Revised Standard Version NRSV). What binds and prevents us from helping ourselves as well as others live in places of peace, love, and joy? What restricts us from walking in faith with a heart that truly says? Yes God, I hear you. Yes God, I'll obey."

Could it be, being taught to put away the sins of the world, we have become preoccupied with looking Holy; while tucking away and ignoring private sins of the heart? Very few persons teach us to recognize, identify, and acknowledge inward pains. These pains have the capability of forming dens of inward iniquity, which result in transgressions against one's self.

Dens of inward iniquity may seem to be a strong statement. But if we consider sin as, "anything that moves us away from who God designed and created us to be" we will view the storehouse of emotional bondage we harbor in different terms. When we act in ways that move us from the glory we were designed to perpetuate; we sin against God and ourselves. We create blockages that limit how, when, where and for what purposes God can use us. Most of the time these actions have become a part of the fiber and fabric of our being. Our lives have been so impacted by our emotional responses that we move in ways that are habitual and harmful. They are harmful because we respond to outside stimuli never considering the condition of our hearts or how our inner being is affected. There is a need in the body of Christ to look within ourselves and find those things that prevent God from propelling us to our destiny.

How many of us as well as persons we minister to accept Christ never associated this salvation with the healing of our inner man? How many of us isolate ourselves from others, overextend ourselves in relationships, or carry anger and bitterness that can be traced to physical, sexual, mental, verbal or emotional abuse that occurred in the past? How many of us have been provoked to think about how our past is impacting our present?

In life when we get hurt, we react to the pain. Our reactions become deterrents to what is best for us at times. Actions based solely on emotional responses, often form habits that become a part of the fabric of our being. For example, as a child I was told that I was nothing and was going to be nothing. As a result, I experienced feelings of rejection, anger, inadequacy, and loneliness. My responses were isolation and a drive to prove, "I am something." I had been made to feel "less than." So my personal purpose became to prove them wrong, "I was worthy of acceptance." I became what some may call an "overachiever", "a perfectionist" or one driven by performance. My life became measured by what I accomplished. On some levels this may be seen as a good thing. I am the one people can count on to get the job done correctly. So what then is the problem? Did God design and call me to be an overachieving perfectionist driven by performance? No! However, those words said to me early in my childhood had an impact that rebounded into my adult life. The emotional response to the pain had a huge impact on the person I was to become. Early on someone's words impacted my inner being and my development as a person. Until I acknowledged this wound and its response, I blocked what God could do in and through me. My actions and reactions were filtered through the emotional trauma I had experienced. Instead of seeing the person I was created to be: one of love, intellect, and strength with a spirit of excellence; I viewed myself in terms of what I could accomplish. This quest of "accomplishing" was an overriding theme. I would perform without a sense of balance or a perception of what my actions were truly costing along the way. My heart was not totally attuned to how and why God would have me answer the call. When this occurs, there is a wedge between God and us that blocks the flow of the Holy Spirit from ministering to and through us in its fullness. We can function and minister with our fears of being rejected, our anger, and our masks of peace. When we do so our emotions become invisible boundaries; keeping those we love and minister to at a distance. Emotional boundaries do not prevent us from living and/or ministering, but greatly impact our lives by decreasing how effective and efficacious we are in relationships. As a result we do not experience life in its fullness.

*"I am come that they might have life, and that they might have it more abundantly."*(John 10:10 KJV).

Abundantly can be seen as growing, experiencing and prospering in those things that are good and bring peace to our spirits. Life in abundance provides a more authentic and intimate connection with the Creator. This connection empowers us to create relationships from a personal place of honesty, authenticity and spiritual integ-

rity. We become more effective when we connect, communicate and share with
others.

We must begin to heal and help others to heal. We must begin to seek and provide opportunities where people can voice their feelings, hurts and pains. This should be done in an atmosphere that addresses these blockages in light of God's word and God's love. We should not cover the pain with cute clichés but really provide individuals with opportunities to explore and move beyond the brokenness that haunts their everyday lives and situations.

There are many different emotional responses that become engrained in our behavior patterns. These responses block us from moving as God designed. The list below identifies some examples of emotions and emotional responses. Both emotions and emotional responses can become blockages to the spirit of God moving in our lives. In viewing this list keep in mind that each individual must pray and ask the Holy Spirit to reveal those things, which prohibit you from walking in the fullness of what God has ordained for your life.

| | | |
|---|---|---|
| rage | cannot receive criticism | blaming |
| excessive fear | inability to be intimate | defensiveness |
| anxiety & panic attacks | depression | isolation |
| self-absorbed | low self esteem | manipulative |
| performance driven | people pleasing | abusive |

| addiction to approval | rescuing others | controlling |
| --- | --- | --- |
| thoughts of suicide | eating disorders | violence |
| gambling addiction | drug & alcohol abuse | perfectionism |
| shopping addiction | attention driven | cutting |
| sexually inappropriate actions | highly critical | pessimistic |

*[Portions of the above list are taken from Terry Wardle's book "Wounded".]*

So, how do we unstop the blockages? We should begin by viewing the process of salvation as an ongoing partner in our lives and homes. Salvation offers us the opportunity to be saved from our grief as well as our sorrows. "Surely He has borne our griefs (sicknesses, weaknesses, and distresses) and carried our sorrows and pains...."(Isaiah 53:4 AMP). God's word acknowledges that salvation encompasses more than our actions. We must begin to acknowledge the same. The salvation that Christ offers encompasses our total well-being, body, soul and spirit.

As we accept God's gift of salvation, we make room for the transformation process to occur. As we grow in Christ, development from the inside out should be prominent. The process of sanctification takes place as we understand and mature in who Christ says we are.

*"For with the heart man believeth unto righteousness; and with the mouth confession is made unto salvation."*(Romans 10:10 KJV). Confession is the key for salvation. Confession prepares the way for salvation to occur. Confession is defined as the

revealing of circumstances; it is to acknowledge, own and admit what is true. Confession is critical criteria in the process of inner healing. Confession surrenders the contents of our hearts to another. Confession provides release and relief. Confession opens the door for cleansing and conversion. Confession in its purest form opens channels that are blocked and allows one to breathe. But what is it that we are confessing to God on a daily, weekly, or even monthly basis? While we are confessing our sins, we should also confess our emotions and the events, which provoked those feelings. Often we are not positioned or provoked to surrender when it comes to personal pain. We should come to God totally surrendering all of ourselves. One holds nothing back in a position of surrender. Most blockages occur because we do not offer up our private innermost feelings to God. We sulk or keep those things privately stored away in our hearts.

    Confession opens the way for God's saving and redemptive power to transform and restore us. Confession restores us to a state of open, honest, innocent communion with God not marred by the harsh realities of life. If our lives are a journey then those things we experience should never detract from life; but rather our experiences should inform and enhance our lives. This begins with open, honest communion with God and ends with persons recognizing that II Corinthians 3:18 is being accomplished in their lives continually. We need to understand that unstopping the blockages is a process that is only possible when we bring our hurts and pains to God. We must acknowledge that we need God to heal the brokenness by surrendering ourselves, totally: body, soul, and spirit. This includes our emotions as well as our mindset. When we surrender, our emotions do not control us but rather guide us into a keen awareness of self.

    Self-awareness sets the atmosphere for open honest communication, which invokes an effective prayer life. Prayer opens the channels for two-way communication to occur between God and us. As we speak God hears. We must believe that God hears. This belief must acknowledge that God is acting on our behalf to bring us to places of healing and wellness both inside and out. Our belief system is critical to the process. *"For with the heart man believeth unto righteousness..."*(Romans. 10:10 KJV). It is important to understand that Romans 10:10 explains that through our belief in him, God will bring us into right standing. Our belief is predicated on the condition of the heart. The heart must know and be confident that God can and will bring healing. This is not predicated by our thoughts (our mind), which can stray depending on how things look or feel. Believing with the heart is being confident that God can and will bring about salvation in one's soul regardless of the circumstances.

    As we offer ourselves to God, there is one other thing we must be willing to do. We must learn to forgive. Un-forgiveness is an emotional response rooted in blame, resent, and punitive action. Forgiveness unveils the seeds of bitterness and control that seek revenge and deny redemption. Removing the veil frees the hand of God to transform and restore us. Forgiveness removes the anger, resentment, and bitterness that can eat away at our souls; blocking us from participating in the transformative process explained in II Corinthians

*"And we, who with unveiled faces all reflect the Lord's glory, are being transformed into his likeness with ever-increasing glory, which comes from the Lord, who is the Spirit."*(II Corinthians 3:18 NIV).

The qualifying factor for transformation is an unveiled face. The unveiling causes a transparency that allows us access to the reflection of God's glory. We must be willing to give up anything that prevents God's glory from being seen in and through us. In doing so, we acknowledge God's purpose and provision for our lives. This position of prostration provokes awareness that God's ear is attuned to us.

    So when we perceive that God does not hear us, perhaps we

should ask the following questions. Could it be that we are not able to effectively communicate? Have we become mute? Are we unable to communicate because we will not be honest with God, surrendering our deepest pains and fears? Have we then, (being mute) decided to medicate our condition with the perception that God has become deaf? Are we holding God hostage to our pain by labeling certain areas in our lives, "no trespassing" zones?

    Unstopping the blockages requires surrender. We must meet God in quiet places of total surrender to remove emotional blockages. Total surrender (body, soul, and mind) disintegrates that blockage that prevents us from moving in the fullness of our callings, our ministries and our everyday lives.

# About The Author

Sandra M. Walker

*Sandra M. Walker, is the founder and Executive Director of Spirit of David Ministries, a Holistic Ministry of Worship, Healing, & Wellness. Spirit of David's mission is to inspire persons to become vessels following after the heart of God. In ministry she teaches that God honors a heart that is loyal before him and that even in midst of our humanity God's love remains steadfast and loyal unto us. She conducts monthly workshops entitled, "In His Image." These workshops endeavor the love, work, and word of God in a way that assists others in developing an intimacy and transparency with God. She believes this is where complete inner healing begins. Sandra is a member of the National Association of Professional Women, holds a Masters of Divinity Degree from Virginia Union University, is a graduate of the Evans Smith Leadership Institute and was awarded an Advanced Certificate in Christian Education. She is sought out by many for her ability to teach the word of God with prophetic revelation and insight. While she is honored to be the mother of three (Jeremiah, Jovan, and Brittney); she is enamored with her role as Grammi to her three beautiful grandchildren: Jared, Jadyn, and Alana. For more information or to book an In His Image Session contact Spirit of David Ministries at whw@spiritofdavid.org or call (800)376-0754. Please visit our website: www.spiritofdavid.org.*

# Chapter 12

## *And He Still Hears*

    As I pondered on what the Lord would have me to say to you, the Lord said tell them I do hear. Often times in life we wonder if God really hears us. When trials come we wonder, how come my situation has not changed? I have been lacking for many years. When am I going to see the over flow that many speak of continually. Think back on the time when you would pray to God and God returned a quick answer to your request. Now you find yourself in a season of wondering and waiting. Did God close His ear to me and if He did why? Could it be that your posture changed and not God's. Could it be that your prayers of thanksgiving have changed into petitions of complaints?

    Instead of praising God your praise has now ceased. Is the intensity of your praise that you display before men the same behind closed doors? God said, don't put on a show for me in public. Don't dance, shout or bow down as a form of humility. Man hears you say God I'm nothing without you. But God hears the pride and arrogance that now pours out from the depths of your heart, due to the anointing He has placed on your life. God says you tell me you love me but yet you despise your brother. When you render praise to God you tell Him how much you love and appreciate Him. However what God hears from the echoes of your heart is the disdain you have against your brother, how can you say you love God but you can't embrace your brother that is near you?

*"Obedience by Faith If someone says, I love God, and hates his brother, he is a liar; for he who does not love his brother whom he has seen, how can[a] he love God whom he has not seen?*
(I John 4:20 NKJV).

My question to you would be how did you approach our heavenly father? Did you come to God in an angry rage in pursuit of revenge? We often question God about other people's blessings. We say Lord you saw what Susie did: Why didn't you punish her? How could you allow her to be blessed? We say to God Jermaine mistreated me and abused me: Why haven't judgment knocked upon his door yet? It seems like they continue to be blessed no matter what the circumstance. God do you hear me? Yet he hears us but we have to learn not to focus on others failures or blessings. Our focus should be on obeying God and living upright before him, God will not go against his word look at what he says in *"You have heard that it was said, 'You shall love your neighbor[ ] and hate your enemy.' But I say to you, love your enemies, bless those who curse you, do good to those who hate you, and pray for those who spitefully use you and persecute you, [ ] that you may be sons of your Father in heaven; for He makes His sun rise on the evil and on the good, and sends rain on the just and on the unjust. For if you love those who love you, what reward have you? Do not even the tax collectors do the same? And if you greet your brethren[ ] only, what do you do more than others? Do not even the tax collectors[ ] do so? Therefore you shall be perfect, just as your Father in heaven is perfect.* (Matthew 5:43-48 NKJV) No matter who wronged you, you still must love, forgive and most of all move on. Why keep unforgivness in your heart? The person who caused the offense has moved on, making you a distant memory to them.

The question we must ask ourselves is not so much is God listening, but rather what does He hear. Approaching the father with harbored feelings of bitterness, hatred, or unforgiveness isn't the way to come to the throne of grace. This behavior could impact God hearing us and His non response. Before we place our request upon the altar of God, we must first lay ourselves on the altar, allowing the light of God to shine through us. Picture how we are prepped when a doctor has made a decision that an x-ray is needed to view a particular area of your body. The x-ray is needed because they saw some abnormal activity and want to get a closer look. We are then asked to remove all that is familiar, our garments that we wore when we came into the doctor's office. We are then concealed with an approved garment to cover us but remain transparent so that light can still pass through it. When we undergo an x-ray through the light of the machine it shows our skeleton form our insides not out outer layers. Let's look at it from a spiritual perspective the protective garment is our fleshy nature. That is how transparent we are when we go before God. He sees how we really feel. He looks beyond the smile, and the kind words. He sees the inner parts which scream I'm wounded, hurt and angry. God sees past our request he sees the motives of our heart. "But the LORD said to Samuel, *"Do not look at his appearance or at his physical stature, because I have refused him. For the LORD does not see as man sees; [ ] for man looks at the outward appearance, but the LORD looks at the heart."* (1 Samuel 16:7 NKJV).

Father do you hear me? God will only respond to us when we come before him with clean hands and a pure heart. *"Who may ascend into the hill of the LORD? Or who may stand in His holy place? He who has clean hands and a pure heart, Who has not lifted up his soul to an idol, Nor sworn deceitfully."* (Psalm 24:3-4 NKJV). We can't be full of rage, revenge, unforgiveness or jealousy. Our first posture is to be honest with ourselves. You are human; admit you were hurt and offended. Being true to ourselves and our emotions is the first step. Don't you know being honest with yourself is being honest with God? Remember he did make us in his image. Then God said, *"Let Us make man in Our image, according to Our likeness; let them have dominion over the fish of the sea, over the birds of the air, and over the cattle, over all[ ] the earth and over every creeping thing that creeps on the earth."*(Genesis 1:26 NKJV) We are truly a reflection of God in the earth. Don't say I forgive you when you truly haven't forgiven. Don't you know when we go before God with a request in prayer, He searches the motives of our hearts first?

Remember the first thing God does is examines our heart. *"The heart is deceitful above all things, And desperately wicked; Who can know it? I, the LORD, search the heart, I test the mind, Even to give every man according to his ways, According to the fruit of his doings."*(Jeremiah 17:9-10 NKJV). God listens to the echoes of our hearts; He hears our innermost thoughts and feelings. When our heart isn't pure, He hears the words we speak against our brother who has offended us. He hears our thoughts of revenge and jealousy. We pray Lord bless them, but God hears our hatred for them instead. We utter words like I have forgiven them Lord, when we haven't truly forgiven them at all. We must realize that we truly need the help of the Holy Spirit we can't do it on our own. When that soft nudge from the Holy Spirit comes and we try to quickly ignore it, receive the conviction God gives to the areas of our life where He is not pleased. Don't ignore his soft nudge. The words we have hidden in our heart which God has been trying to pluck out for years, offenses we have held against those whom we esteemed highly and were greatly disappointed and hurt. Holding those offenses grieves the very heart of God. The purpose of the holy spirit, which is God's extension in the earth is to heal those wounded areas.

We must be honest with God. Speak to Him and say; Lord I haven't been able to let this thing go, I need you to remove the plague within my heart. Plague as it pertains to our physical heart, is described as hardness around our arteries and can cause a blockage? Unforgivness, with no repentance can cause a blockage. It can cause a wall to rise between us and God. We don't need to just focus on what was done to us. We must also look inwardly and examine ourselves to see if we caused harm to others, which can create a blockage as well. Who have we offended and hurt? Did you reconcile with your brother whom you may have hurt? The bible speaks in the Book of Matthew *"Therefore if you bring your gift to the altar, and there remember that your brother has something against you, leave your gift there before the altar, and go your way. First be reconciled to your brother, and then come and offer your gift."*(Matthew 5:23-24 NKJV). We must allow the blockages within our heart to be removed and our arteries repaired. This must be done so the blood within can flow freely. This is symbolic to the free flow of his spirit through us. When we pray to our father in heaven the words we speak out and the words God hears from the echoes of our heart won't differ but speak exactly the same. These words of peace love and hope, not just for ourselves but others as well. We must receive the words of healing and restoration for ourselves first then our families and then others. We have to make sure we are approaching our God in true humility and not false humility, the father knows the difference believe that! We must not act prideful or boastful. Remember there is nothing good in our flesh. *"For I know that in me (that is, in my flesh) nothing good dwells; for to will is present with me, but how to perform what is good I do not find."*(Romans 7:18 NKJV). This is why we must place ourselves on the altar daily.

    God is saying to us yes I hear you, but I don't like what I'm hearing. I am hearing more words of cursing than of blessing; more judgments of others than of yourselves. Stop telling on everyone one else, start telling me more about you. I desire to use you, but my lack of response is due to what I am hearing.

    By all means don't allow jealousy to take route. Jealousy can come in many forms, when we see others get blessed. You may ask, I have been faithful why not me instead of them? If you're not careful not only will jealousy show up, but the spirit of competition will rise as well. Looks can be deceiving in so many ways. Don't get caught up in the perception of a blessing, make sure it is a blessing from the Lord, and by all means don't compete.

When we are praying to God remember to make sure He is hearing your sincerity, your love for Him and most of all your need for him. God will not respond to a grievous request. Think about it this way, I don't like to argue or listen to arguments. If you are like me if someone is arguing with you and especially if they are screaming, you can be present and shut them out. In other words tune them out, and you will remain in that posture until their voice calms and the attacks have stopped. Another example is when you have made up within your mind about something or someone, and someone comes along and tries to change your mind. No matter what is said your thoughts about that something or someone does not change. Well God is that way when we come to him unrepented of our wrong, wishing punishments upon others, wanting famine and drought to hit their household, God turns a deaf ear to our request. God knows the inner parts of man. We don't know the inner parts unless God reveals it to us.

Sometimes we find ourselves in a place of frustration, wondering when God will respond to what we consider is an urgent request. Awaiting God's response is the hardest part for us as believers. Grandma always told us the Lord will make away somehow. He is never late but always on time. Hearing it and believing it is two different things. We often ask, Lord why is it taking so long! I'm tired of this same situation. Why haven't you moved yet? Do you really trust God with your life? Think on that for a minute. If we truly trust God with our lives and truly believe He hears us then we wouldn't become so anxious. For example we question why it's taking so long, but the mere fact we ask that question audibly or within our mind, lets us know we have become focused on time. We have placed God within our timeline, even though he is a timeless God. We have set up a timetable of when we expect God to move. When we are waiting on the Lord we must do away with our timeline. I believe in the midst of waiting we need to take that time to go through a self check. What is it about us that need to change? What are we waiting for? God doesn't only come to change our circumstances and situations. God comes to change and empower us to bring transformation to our own circumstances and situations. Remember when we have received Jesus Christ as our Lord and Savior, He now abides inside of us. *"You are of God, little children, and have overcome them, because He who is in you is greater than he who is in the world."* (1 John 4:4 NKJV).

We are eager to see the true manifestations of God come to past, but before we can see true manifestation which are our dreams and desires inspired by God. We must allow God to change us first. What are we waiting on God to do? Is it something that we can do ourselves? What is your attitude like while you are waiting on God? Don't let the enemy deceive you into thinking that God doesn't care and that your waiting is in vain. Don't believe the lie. God cares about you so much so that he has an account for every hair on you head. *"Are not two sparrows sold for a copper coin? And not one of them falls to the ground apart from your Father's will. But the very hairs of your head are all numbered. Do not fear therefore; you are of more value than many sparrows."* (Matthew 10:29-31 NKJV). You are so valuable to God; don't clam up because God has not responded YET. Don't you know your destiny has already been mapped out by God? Before you were even conceived God already knew who you were and ordered your steps. Don't allow confusion of where you feel you should be in life be distract you from where you are going in life. The bible tell us in *"Then the word of the LORD came to me, saying: Before I formed you in the womb I knew you; Before you were born I sanctified you; I ordained you a prophet to the nations."* (Jeremiah 1:4-5 NKJV). Your destiny has already been determined the good the bad and the ugly. I don't care what you have done know that it will all work together for you good. *"And we know that all things work together for good to those who love God, to those who are the called according to His purpose."*(Romans 8:28 NKJV).

      Move past the hurt and pain of your past. God heard you when you said Lord forgive me and you meant it. He is aware of your shortcomings. We are working towards perfection but are yet not perfected. Be mindful of what you really feel in your heart. Allow God to truly purge you of all uncleanness. If we could clean ourselves up I think we would have done it by now. Pay attention to what God has shared with us about what he hears when we don't repent or forgive. Let's allow God to work through us his purposes and plans for our lives. Let it all go. It's time to go forth in purpose and power. God hears and knows and will not allow your peace to ever be broken. Let's mediate on the things outlined in Philippians. *"Meditate on These Things. Finally, brethren, whatever things are true, whatever things are noble, whatever things are just, whatever things are pure, whatever things are lovely, whatever things are of good report, if there is any virtue and if there is anything praiseworthy—meditate on these things. The things which you learned and received and heard and saw in me, these do, and the God of peace will be with you."*(Philippians 4:8-9 NKJV). My prayer is as you have read the pages of this book that you allowed God to search you, purge you, and make you new. And most of all that you realize He Still Hears.

## Lets Pray

*Father God as I humble myself before you, I know that I am nothing without you. I ask first for your forgiveness for not letting go of my past hurt and negative experiences; for not truly being honest first with myself and then with you. I believe your word when it said I am made in your image and likeness. God I desire to be more like you. Remove what needs to be removed from me inwardly, and outwardly in my relationship with others. Pull the weeds out of my life that comes to destroy my purpose and destiny in you. Let me truly love my brother the way you love me. Teach me how to trust you more and most of all wait on you. Help me not to doubt that you hear me. I come against the lies of the devil that says "I'm worthless and you don't care". I will not walk in confusion but in peace. Please fill me with your spirit again; I recommit my life to you this day. I thank you God for the blood of Jesus which covers me. Thank you for your forgiveness, your unconditional love towards me and for remaining the same and never changing. Thank you for never turning your back on me and most of all never giving up on me. But most of all Lord I thank you for listening to me. It is in Jesus Name I Pray Amen!*

# About The Author

Pastor Trena Stephenson

*Pastor Trena Stephenson is an ordained Pastor. She is serving under the awesome leadership of Apostle June A. Hunter - founder and administrator of ATOM (Agape Teas Outreach Ministries) of Petersburg, VA. She is also the Pastor, Founder and President of Woman of God Ministries, Inc. which is a 501(c) 3 non-profit organization established to bring women into the fullness of what God has for them and their ministries. Pastor Trena is the CEO/Founder of Daughters of Distinction which was formed to create a medium for Women of God to pursue their dreams as it pertains to writing, television, and audio publications. Daughters of Distinction were formed in 2007 and now house an awesome staff of Women of God that holds the same passions as our upcoming authors. Pastor Trena is a gifted preacher, teacher, worship leader, author, playwright and intercessor. To learn more about this awesome woman of God log onto. www.wofgod.org and www.dofdllc.com.*

## *How it all began......*

Well dear readers the Lord prompted me to share how this book came to fruition. This seed was planted in my life about two years ago, during a time of much pain and sorrow; I was still trying to recover from about 4 years of constant life storms. I had lost 2 different jobs due to downsizing in a three year period. Just when I would recover from one job loss here comes another loss.
During this time our nation had just entered into a mortgage crisis which impacted me greatly. Due to my lack of employment, I lost my home to foreclosure. My daughter and I had to move in with a friend. You couldn't have told me before the storm hit that I would ever find myself in that type of dilemma; I was doing pretty well not really wanting for anything. If that wasn't enough my marriage ended as well. I found myself in so much despair, but the Lord told me to start a publishing group called "Daughters of Distinction." God told me He wanted me to compose a book and call it "And He Still Hears." This book will be the first of many books birthed out from this company the Lord has establish through me. I know why God told me to share this with our readers, because many of you who have read the pages from this book are full of dreams and visions. Yes, you can do it and your time has now come! Purpose and destiny is birth through pain. All you have to do is think of the process of childbirth. I just want to say to you -go through your process as painful as it may be even when you feel like giving up don't. There is a purpose and plan for your life. I can speak from a personal stand point. I felt like giving up, I battled depression and even loss my will to live at times but as hard as it was when God spoke I started my process in preparing for this moment. I got my

strength back through prayer, reading his word and I focused on his promises. God didn't make a mistake when he made me. There was more he required of me. I had to endure what I went through so I could be a blessing and most of all an example of His faithfulness and love before others. If He said it He will perform it. Hold on don't allow your dreams and visions die. Your destiny and purpose will be fulfilled. As you have read the pages of this book know that it comes from the very heart of God to bring correction, encouragement and most of all change. This book is a testament to what God will do through a willing vessel that is sold out. The seed that was planted over two years ago has now been birthed out. It's now your time to give birth.

I love you more than you will ever know

Trena

# SADIQA'S PLACE: A HOUSE OF HOPE (SPAHOH)
ciaministries@aol.com
443-708-0321

---

The women of SPAHOH are women you work with every day and may not ever know it. Many of the women have experienced abusive relationships and feel that they have no place to go or no one to turn to; and others were at one time incarcerated, or were homeless living in abandoned housing. These women have all had challenges in life, and because of their inappropriate choices coupled with their inability to deal with situations several of them used drugs and alcohol or both of these substances to mask their pain.

The vision of SPAHOH is to eradicate homelessness, a social barrier, for women, and children by creating a unique supportive housing program, while working collaboratively with a variety of transitional services agencies.

This vision began as a result of the trials, tests and tribulations in my life. As I look back over my life and recall the days of homelessness, being a drug addicted woman with a child, who was in need of direction, but had no direction to offer myself much less a child. Making wrong decisions I found myself living from house to house looking for someone to love and care for me--to take care of me. With no one to really love me, I took my hurt, pain and disappointments of life and wrapped them in the temporary comfort and peace of mind that I found in drugs, but it was only temporary. No family, no friends, my world was falling apart. I lost my house, my car and my job. Like the prodigal son, I returned home to Baltimore only to discover that family was not there for me. I didn't receive the open arms of welcome home and a party like the prodigal son, but shut doors and looks of "what a shame."

After the humility factor of seeking others for a place to live, with no money in hand, it was a very short stay and consequently I ended up having to sleep in my car, thus, the mission and compassion for Sadiqa's Place: A House of Hope (SPAHOH) was birthed, --To provide women, who are homeless, with supportive housing and transitional services that will afford them the opportunity to get their life back on track, with a renewed outlook on life.

The women of SPAHOH, like me, often ask these questions: "How did I get here?" and more importantly "How do I overcome the situation I find myself in?" Admitting that I was powerless over a few things and surrendering my life to Christ was the best thing I ever did. I have a passion to help other women to discover their God given abilities and gifts and to use them to help someone else make it to the other side of through. I know now that nothing is impossible with Christ and that all things work together for good to them that love the Lord—and Love Him I do.

*Some of the proceeds from this book will go to help the vision of SPAHOH.*

## *Upcoming Releases from Daughters of Distinction*

Introducing the Series Entitled "The Fullness of God"

I.   And He Still Hears

II.  And He Still Speaks is due to be released February 2011

III. And He Still Sees is due to be release June 2011

IV.  And He Still Waits is due to be released December 2011

To learn more about the services and upcoming releases go to www.dofdllc.com

# References

Ogilvie, Lloyd John. Lord of the Impossible. Nashville: Abingdon Press, 1984

Hagee, John. Life's Challenges Your Opportunity. Lake Mary: Charisma House, 2009.

Hill, Richard J. "What Does God Know and Why Does He Know It?" Glimpse of Grace. n.d.
Accessed on 17 June 2010. <http://www.glimpsesofgrace.org/html/foreknowledge.html>.

"Omniscient." Merriam-Webster Online Dictionary. 2010. Merriam-Webster Online. 17 June 2010. <http://www.merriam-webster.com/dictionary/omniscient>

"Common Skin and Nail Conditions?" American Podiatric Medical Association. 19 May 2009.
Accessed on 30 June 2010. <http://www.apma.org/Members/PracticeManagement/Marketing/Customizable- PowerPoint>.

"Hate." Merriam-Webster Online Dictionary. 2010. Merriam-Webster Online. 30 June 2010. <http://www.merriam-webster.com/dictionary/hate>

"Lebab." Strong's Hebrew Dictionary. 2004-2010. Strong's Hebrew Dictionary Online. 15 June 2010. <http://www.strongsnumbers.com/hebrew/3824.htm>.

"Yada." Strong's Hebrew Dictionary. 2004-2010. Strong's Hebrew Dictionary Online. 15 June 2010. <http://www.strongsnumbers.com/hebrew/3045.htm>.

"Pruning." Merriam-Webster Online Dictionary. 2010. Merriam-Webster Online. 30 June 2010. <http://www.merriam-webster.com/dictionary/pruning>

"Trippin." Urban Dictionary.com. 1999-2010. Urban Dictionary Online. 15 June 2010. <http://www.urbandictionary.com>.

"Self-Control." Merriam-Webster Online Dictionary. 2010. Merriam-Webster Online. 17 June 2010. <http://www.merriam-webster.com/dictionary/self-control>

"Threshing." Merriam-Webster Online Dictionary. 2010. Merriam-Webster Online. 17 June 2010. <http://www.merriam-webster.com/dictionary/threshing>

Miles, C. Austin. "Garden of Prayer Hymn." Adam Geibel Publisher, 1912.

Roberts, Frances J. Come Away My Beloved. Uhrichsville: Barbour Publishing Inc, 1973.

Wardle, Terry. Wounded. Abilene: Leafwood Publishers, 1994.

"Confess." Random House Online Dictionary. 2010 Random House Online 6 June 2010. <http://dictionary.reference.com/browse/confess>.

www.ingramcontent.com/pod-product-compliance
Lightning Source LLC
Chambersburg PA
CBHW041305110426
42743CB00037B/1